THE DREAM TRAVELER'S
Game
THE BOY AND HIS SONG

THE DREAM TRAVELER'S SERIES
—— BOOK 5 ——

TED DEKKER & H.R. HUTZEL

ISBN 979-8-9865173-8-4 (Paperback Edition)

Also available in the Dream Travelers Game series

The Warrior and the Archer (Book 6)
ISBN 979-8-9865173-9-1 (Paperback Edition)

Out of the Darkness (Book 7)
ISBN 979-8-9888509-0-8 (Paperback Edition)

Also available in the Dream Travelers Quest series (the prequel)

Into the Book of Light (Book 1)
ISBN 978-0-9968124-6-7 (Paperback Edition)

The Curse of Shadow Man (Book 2)
ISBN 978-0-9968124-7-4 (Paperback Edition)

The Garden and the Serpent (Book 3)
ISBN 978-0-9968124-8-1 (Paperback Edition)

The Final Judgement (Book 4)
ISBN 978-0-9968124-9-8 (Paperback Edition)

Published by:
Scripturo
PO Box 2618
Keller, Texas 76248

Cover art and design by Manuel Preitano

Printed in the United States of America

Chapter One

THEO PUSHED A BUTTERY BROCCOLI floret across his plate, then poked at a filet of salmon.

"Fish again?" he asked without looking up.

"I thought you liked salmon, dear," his grandmother said. She entered the small dining area from the kitchen, carrying a pitcher of lemon water. "It's good for you." She filled his glass, then took the seat across from him. "Besides, you can hardly live in Florida and not have fish at least once a week."

He glanced up at her, seeing her warm smile, but her soft blue eyes held a hint of sadness behind the thin rims of her glasses. "I can make you something else if you'd prefer."

"No, it's fine. I mean, it's great. Thanks, Grandma."

"You're welcome, dear." She held out her hand. "You want to say grace tonight?"

Theo placed his hand against her weathered palm. "You can do it."

She held his gaze for a long moment, then closed her eyes and recited the familiar prayer.

Theo's eyes drifted past her and landed on the photograph of his father on the wall, displayed with prominence in the entryway right before the kitchen entry. His mother's photo hung on the wall directly across from it. Theo traced his father's familiar smile with his eyes, remembering that today was Thursday. The two of them would be ordering pizza and watching their favorite TV show right about now—if his father were here.

"Amen," his grandmother said, interrupting his thoughts. She squeezed Theo's hand, then released it. "Let's dig in," she said, a little too excitedly for such a healthy meal.

Theo popped a piece of broccoli into his mouth.

"So, how was school today?"

"Fine."

"Just fine?" She watched him chew. "It's your fresh-man year. Surely there must be something exciting you can share with your grandmother."

Theo shoved a bite of salmon into his mouth so he wouldn't have to answer right away. He glanced across the open room to the large picture window at the back of the house. Fading sunlight glimmered on the large pond in the backyard. He remembered the time he and his dad had attempted paddleboarding on it shortly after they'd moved in with his grandmother. It had been one of his dad's last "good days." Theo swallowed the fish, trying to come up with anything he could share about his school day that came close to the joy he'd felt while watching his father fall off his board and splash into the water.

Pressure formed behind his eyes. He blinked, then faced his grandmother.

"Just a normal school day."

She set down her fork, took a sip of water, then leaned back in her chair. "Theo, do you think it might be a good idea to start seeing your therapist again?" She paused. "It's been eight months since your dad passed … And I know everyone grieves differently—in their own time and in their own way—and it's okay to still be sad, but—" She hesitated. "I'm worried about you."

Theo turned to look out the window again, watching the fronds of the palm trees sway in the evening breeze.

"You don't have to worry," he said. "I'll be okay."

She was silent for a long moment before asking, "So do you want me to make an appointment for you with the therapist?"

"No." He forced a smile and looked her in the eyes. "Thanks for asking, though."

She pressed her lips together. "Do you mind if I ask why you don't want to go back?"

Theo shrugged, then poked at another piece of broccoli with his fork. "I guess it's like you said. I'm grieving in my own way. Therapy wasn't that helpful."

That and his therapist just wanted to put him on medication. The doctor had prescribed two different antidepressant prescriptions before finally listening to Theo when he said the medicine made him feel worse than he felt without it. He stopped seeing the therapist shortly thereafter.

Theo's phone buzzed in his pocket. The vibration sounded louder than normal in the otherwise silent house.

His grandmother picked up her fork again. "Is that a message from one of your friends?"

Theo heard the hint of hope in her question.

"Go ahead. You can answer it." She was always encouraging Theo to make new friends. Though he'd been living in Florida for a little over a year, he had a tough time connecting with the kids at his school.

Theo and his dad had moved in with Theo's grandmother shortly after his father was diagnosed with pancreatic cancer. She and Theo helped care for his father in his final days, which left little time for making new friends, even if he had been in the emotional and mental state to do so. Then after his dad passed, Theo had chosen to fill his time with video games. After all, a game never asked him how he was doing—a question Theo hated to answer.

He pulled his phone from his pocket and read the notification on the home screen.

Annelee: Hey, haven't heard from you in a while. How's Florida? You free to chat tonight?

Theo unlocked his phone and opened the text messaging app.

He had nine messages from Annelee over the past month, and he hadn't responded to any of them.

"Well?" his grandma said with a smile in her voice. "Who is it? A girl maybe?"

Theo dimmed the home screen and returned the phone to his pocket. "Just someone from my old school."

"Oh. Well, okay then." She waited for him to continue. When he didn't, she reverted her attention to her meal, allowing a familiar silence to settle between them.

Theo picked at his food, his mind drifting to his days with Annelee, Danny, and Asher, almost three years ago.

It was strange to think about it now because it felt so distant. Like an unbelievable dream. But it had happened, hadn't it? At least they were positive it had happened back then. Using an ancient book called the Book of History, which they'd found in a secret room in the school library, they'd traveled to another dimension. There, in a magical land, they'd gone on a quest to find the Five Seals of Truth, and as each seal was found, marks had appeared on their shoulders like tattoos.

But that seemed so long ago now, and a lot had happened since then.

For the first three months after returning from their quest, Theo and his friends had met daily in the library to talk about their adventures. The lessons they'd learned in the other world and the burning truth of the seals on their arms consumed their thoughts and conversations. Their experiences had changed them— all four of them.

But soon the tattoolike marks on their arms faded, dimming with each passing day, until they were nothing more than a distant memory. Still, Theo and his friends met regularly to remind themselves of the seals.

Then Mrs. Friend, the librarian, transferred to a different school, and the mystical Book of History which they'd used to travel between worlds disappeared with her.

A few months later, Asher's father accepted a position as the head principal at a high school in North

Dakota, and they moved. Theo, Annelee, and Danny continued to meet once a week. Though the seals had vanished from their arms, the marks and their meanings still branded their hearts. The sage from Other Earth, Talya, had warned them that remembering would be their greatest challenge and they were determined to never forget.

But over time, the wonder surrounding their transformation had dimmed. The details of their journey had grown foggy. Theo's adventures in Other Earth started to feel less like a memory and more like a story he'd read.

When Danny transferred out of foster care and moved into his permanent adoptive home in another state, it became even more challenging to keep the memories alive.

Then, a year and a half after their quest in Other Earth, Theo's dad received his diagnosis and his world flipped upside down.

The cancer had been aggressive, stealing his father's life in ten short months.

In the days following his dad's death, Theo had cried out to God, to the guides he'd met in Other Earth—to anyone who would listen and help him see through his pain. But the only response he received was silence. Theo began to wonder if maybe he really had only dreamed of his adventures in Other Earth.

In the weeks after the funeral, Theo had received text messages from all three of his friends. They checked in on him regularly, but Theo didn't know how to respond. So he didn't. Eventually, Danny and Asher stopped reaching out. Only Annelee continued to text Theo.

The sound of his grandmother's fork hitting her plate jolted Theo from his thoughts.

"All finished, dear?" She gestured to his half-eaten meal.

"I'm just not that hungry tonight."

She nodded. "I'll take your plate." She held out a hand.

Theo pushed back from his chair, stood, and cleared both his plate and hers. He kissed his grandma on the cheek. "You cooked, so I'll do the dishes. Thanks for dinner."

She turned in her chair, watching him walk into the kitchen and begin loading the dishwasher.

"You're such a sweet boy, Theo."

He peered over the bar-height counter and forced another smile in her direction, ignoring the vibrating buzz of his phone in his pocket.

Theo rolled over in his bed and stared at the dark ceiling. He pulled his phone off his nightstand, unlocked it, and opened Annelee's messages.

Annelee: Hey. Did you get my message? Want to chat tonight?

She'd sent the message at 6:43 p.m.

Theo glanced at the time in the top left-hand corner of the phone screen.

10:52 p.m.

It was certainly too late to chat now—not that he had something to say. He touched his finger to the reply section and started typing.

Hey. Sorry. Was eating dinner with my grandma when you texted …

He stopped, erased his reply, and stared at the screen.

Hey. Nice to hear from you. It's been a while. Maybe we can try to chat …

He deleted the text and dimmed his phone, tossing it onto the bed beside him.

Sighing, he sat up, frustrated that his algebra homework hadn't lulled him to sleep as he'd hoped. He flicked on the side-table lamp, eyes scanning the sparse space. It was much smaller than his bedroom at his old house—so small, in fact, it fit little more than the queen-size bed, nightstand, and dresser.

A few of his old posters stood rolled up in the corner, leaning against the dresser. He'd thought about hanging the Vanisher poster, but he never got around to it. After his father had passed, he wanted as few reminders as possible of his old life. Still, every once in a while, Theo would unroll the poster and stare at the images from his childhood.

After kicking off the blankets, Theo crossed the room to his dresser and flicked on the small TV and PlayStation that sat on top of it. He grabbed the controller and TV remote, climbed back into bed, then quickly turned down the volume so he wouldn't wake his grandma.

Leaning back against the headboard, he clicked his profile on the screen—*Dream Traveler_2643*—then started scrolling through his game options. Theo's PlayStation wasn't the latest console—his grandma had bought it used after his dad had passed—but it was certainly better than the old gaming system he'd had back home.

He paused on one of the games. *Journey to Impossible Places: The Viren Chronicles ...* He frowned. "I don't remember downloading that." He leaned forward and examined the game's thumbnail cover image—a majestic fantasy city amid a bright green landscape. The silhouette of a player stood in the foreground, while a large white bird—an owl maybe—swooped through the sky in the background. The title of the game scrolled across the image in an elaborate gold font.

Theo shrugged. "Looks cool." He clicked the image. The screen dimmed blue, then came to life with the opening credits and narration.

An aged map unfolded on the screen, lined with fading ink and inscriptions. Theo scanned the drawings of mountains to the north and opposing forests in the west and east. A long river cut across the map, running north and south.

The screen zoomed in toward the center of the map, focusing on a walled city labeled the Kingdom of Viren. As the drawing grew larger, the yellowed paper faded, replaced with colored animation depicting a fantasy cityscape.

The soft timbre of the narrator's voice played through the speakers over cinematic music.

"Long ago in a faraway land, there was a beautiful green-glassed city called Viren, governed by the wise and noble King Tyrus. The city was a peaceful and enviable place to dwell."

The screen zoomed out from the city and panned east over the river until it reached a black forest. A mountain loomed in the distance.

"But one day, a dark stranger appeared in the land, seeking audience with the king. He kidnapped the king's daughter and poisoned Tyrus's mind, transforming him into a dark tyrant who now rules the land with fear."

The screen panned over the world once more, drifting past the walled city in the center, scanning north over a mountainous region, then traveling far west and pausing over a deep green forest. The narrator continued, "A rebel group escaped the city, fleeing with their lives and the hope of rescuing the princess and restoring the Kingdom of Viren to its former glory."

The screen descended through the canopy of trees and settled at ground level, panning side to side to reveal dense vegetation. A flicker of white appeared in the distance between two trees.

"You are invited to join their mission—to rescue the princess and liberate the king and city from the dark stranger's curse before it's too late."

The white flicker in the distance drew closer, and a glimmering gold button appeared on the screen, emblazoned with the words *Play Now*.

"Hmm…" Theo mumbled.

Using his controller, he clicked. The gold button disappeared, but the white object in the background continued to draw near. Theo navigated through trees, seeing the entire forest through a first-person point of view. He moved toward the white object, then squinted. It looked like it might be the owl from the cover image. But now its features looked more batlike. It hobbled straight toward him, waving a winged arm in greeting. Using his controller, Theo approached. Soon, the image of the giant, fluffy white creature filled the screen. It blinked with bright-green eyes.

Theo froze and set the controller down. The bat looked unsettlingly familiar.

It waved at him again, this time in a beckoning motion, then stepped closer. It pressed its hand against the screen. Theo felt blood drain from his face. He slid from his bed to the floor and crossed to the TV.

Again, the bat motioned for him to come, then returned its hand to the glass from the inside.

"This is so weird," Theo said under his breath. "I've never seen a game like this before."

Yet as he said the words, a thought flickered through his mind. Maybe he *had* played a game like this.

The bat's green eyes followed Theo as he stepped closer to the screen, then held his gaze. The cinematic music crescendoed in the background, and the bat raised its fluffy white eyebrows as if asking an unspoken question.

Theo hesitated, then reached out. He touched a

finger to the TV screen. The bat turned its head, watching Theo move. The smooth, cool surface gave way beneath his touch, and Theo's finger passed through the screen.

He yanked his hand back and stared at it.

On the screen, the bat grinned, lifted its palm, then pressed it on the exact spot Theo had touched.

A lightheaded feeling washed over him. He inched closer, placing his entire palm on the screen, lining it up with the creature's small hand.

Theo's fingers sank into the flat surface as if they were passing through water.

Warmth enveloped his hand along with a soft buzz.

The bat flashed a grin and winked.

The bat's fingers locked around Theo's wrist and pulled.

With a gasp, Theo felt himself being sucked into the screen—not just his hand and arm but his whole body.

Before he could stop himself, he was falling into the game.

Chapter Two

THEO'S BODY PLUMMETED, smacking tree branches as he fell. He landed hard on his back and groaned, staring up at the sunlight streaming through the canopy of trees. The hum of insects and chirp of birds greeted him. Pressing his hands into the soft soil, he pushed up and scanned his surroundings. He sat in a forest that looked exactly like the one in the game.

Theo rubbed the back of his neck, then stood. "This can't be possible." He examined his hands. "It has to be a dream."

A strange and familiar sensation washed over him. He shook his head, feeling a tickle of déjà vu in the back of his mind.

His thoughts drifted to the white bat who had seemingly pulled him through the TV screen and into the game. The creature was nowhere in sight. Theo chuckled to himself, realizing how absurd the whole event sounded.

He sighed with relief. "I'm definitely dreaming."

Something whizzed past Theo's head and smacked into the nearest tree. He turned to see an arrow protruding from the trunk. Eyes wide, he spun to find a cloaked man fifty feet way, pulling a second arrow from his quiver. The man nocked the arrow, drew back on the bowstring, and took aim.

Theo turned and sprinted.

"Halt!" the man shouted.

Thick vegetation grasped at Theo's legs, but he didn't slow his pace.

Another arrow whizzed past him. He darted left and ran faster, not knowing where he was going but desperate to put distance between him and the cloaked archer. The sound of horse's hooves pounded the ground behind him.

A different voice called to him this time. "You there! Halt!"

Theo ignored the command, not daring to stop long enough to find out who was chasing him or what they wanted.

He sprinted toward a denser part of the forest and rushed between two trees. The ground sloped. Theo skidded to a stop, but the loose soil gave way beneath his Converse sneakers. He swung his arms to regain his balance but failed and tumbled down the steep embankment.

Groaning, he rolled to a stop in a dry creek bed.

"There he is!"

Theo stared up at the top of the hill where he'd stood just seconds ago. Through the trees, he saw two cloaked men approaching on horses, one of them gripping a bow.

"I said halt!" the man shouted.

Theo jumped to his feet and dashed across the creek, desperate to find cover again before the archer had a clear shot.

"It's too steep to follow," he heard one of the men shout. "Cut him off at the pass!"

Theo didn't look back but heard the horses retreat. Seeing the faint marks of a game trail to the right, he ducked back into the thick of the forest, dodging thorny vines that swiped at his arms and face.

Twenty yards in, the trees thinned, revealing a clearing. Theo pushed forward, urged on by nothing but adrenaline, blind fear, and an odd instinct that this was the direction he should run. He pulled to a stop as he entered the clearing. In the center sat a white circular structure, the size of a small house, topped with a copper dome that gleamed in the sunlight.

Voices spilled out of the forest. Theo sprinted toward the strange object, hoping it would offer somewhere to hide.

As he drew near to it, Theo couldn't help but feel intrigued by its appearance. White Grecian columns encircled the outer wall, covered in black snaking vines. His pace slowed as he approached, and yet, he felt drawn to it.

Voices sounded behind him again, this time closer. Theo rounded the side of the structure, searching for a door, a window, any way for him to get in and take cover. When he reached the other side of the building, he could hear the clomp of hooves. He ducked in between two of the pillars and pressed his back against the building, realizing they would discover him in seconds. But when his skin contacted the smooth exterior, the surface moved. Theo turned as a massive doorway appeared. The doors swung open. Darkness greeted him. He swallowed and hesitated.

"Elijah!" a voice shouted. "Check that field. Surely he couldn't have gone far."

Theo drew a deep breath and without another second of hesitation stepped into the building.

The doors closed behind him, leaving him in complete darkness.

A subtle humming sound filled his ears, then a whir like a machine booting up. Soft lights flickered on, dimly illuminating the space. Their brightness grew with each passing second. Theo took a step forward, then turned. The door he'd entered was gone, replaced by a smooth white wall. He grazed his fingers against the panel, but nothing happened.

He turned back around to examine the interior, blinking as the lights reached their peak intensity and reflected off the white walls. The building seemed smaller on the inside, the space no bigger than his grandma's living room and kitchen combined. He noted the metallic silver counter that partially lined the perimeter of the round room. A row of display screens hovered above it, all of them glowing a soft shade of green with a loading bar in the center of their display. Theo swallowed. It looked like the control room in a sci-fi spacecraft.

He approached the desk, noticing the keyboards, buttons, and touch pads. The loading bar on each screen hovered at 67 percent. He trailed a finger over the cool stainless-steel desk, careful not to bump any buttons as he walked the perimeter. The long counter ended directly across from the spot where he'd entered the building. A rounded bump-out protruded from the wall and divided the command center into two symmetrical half-moon sections. From what Theo could tell, the bump-out was another room, the size of a large walk-in closet. An intricate white paneled door sat in the center of the protrusion with two pillars on either side. He stared at the door for a long moment, noting that it had no handle or knob. He traced the etching carved into the wood, feeling that same sense of déjà vu wash over him.

Directly above the door hung a large circular shield consisting of a thin white line encircling a green band. Black filled the middle, and a vibrant red cross slashed across the center. A single white dot pierced the cross-bars' intersection, like a nail holding the pieces together.

Theo couldn't pull his eyes from the shield. "White," he murmured. "Green, black, red, and… white. The five seals of truth."

His mind swirled with faint memories he'd put to rest with his childhood fantasies and games. Instinctively, he touched his shoulder, recalling the seals that had once branded his arm. The shield was a replica of those seals.

"A dream," he whispered. "Just like this."

He dropped his hand from his shoulder, once again feeling the sharp stab of pain as he remembered the moment his father had died. The moment Theo had called out to those friends from Other Earth, which he concluded had to be imaginary. How had he, Annelee, Danny, and Asher managed to create a fantasy world that felt so real?

He didn't know.

Tightness formed in Theo's throat as he considered the cruel joke his own mind played on him now. Why would he dream of these things again? Why eight months after the death of his father?

And why on earth would those dreams now mingle with images from *Star Trek*?

Theo placed a hand on his stomach. "I knew that salmon tasted funny."

His eyes drifted past the shield to the white, domed ceiling. It reminded him of the inside of the Jefferson Memorial that he'd seen on his eighth-grade trip to Washington, DC. Theo chewed the inside of his lip, remembering how his father had attended as a chaperone. He blinked, then noticed an inscription that encircled the room just beneath the spot where the dome began. Theo's eyes traced the engraved lettering, but before he could read it, the sound of a dinging chime filled the room. Theo turned to see the loading bar on each screen at 100 percent, and the words *Loading Complete* beneath it.

He stepped toward the nearest screen and waited to see what would happen. The loading bar disappeared as the green screen faded to black.

Another sound filled the room. The sound of a door hissing open.

And then a voice.

"Hello, Theo."

Theo spun back to face the white door. It hissed closed.

A man stood in front of it. There was something familiar about his long white beard and kind eyes. He gripped a large wooden staff in his knobby fingers. A long brown robe draped his thin shoulders; a cord belted it at his waist. Theo met the man's stare. His smile unleashed a flood of memories in Theo's mind until suddenly the man's name was on his tongue.

"Talya?"

The man pushed a strand of his long white hair from his face, then winked at Theo.

Chapter Three

THEO SHOOK HIS HEAD. Not knowing what else to say, he repeated the man's name. "Talya?"

The man took a step toward Theo. "It has been many years, my friend. Three to be exact."

Theo blinked. "I don't understand. You're here? You're real?"

"Of course I'm real," Talya said with a chuckle. "What? Have you forgotten me?"

Theo stared into the man's smiling eyes. He hadn't forgotten Talya, yet at the same time, he had. Because it had all been a dream.

Talya's smile dimmed. "Ah, yes. I can see you have forgotten. Just as I suspected you would."

A memory flickered through Theo's mind, the sound of this man's voice repeating the word *remember*.

Theo straightened his shoulders. "Where am I?"

Talya's smile returned. "Why, in a game, of course."

Theo's eyes scanned the room. "A game?"

The old man gave a swift nod.

"But that's not possible."

"No?" Talya tilted his head to one side. "But you were in a book once. Is that not possible?"

Theo stumbled backward, bumping his lower back into the command center desk. He turned to see a faint reflection of himself in the nearest darkened screen.

He turned back to face Talya. "So that was real. The Book of History? Other Earth? The Roush? All of it?"

Talya held up a hand and chuckled. "Slow down. And yes—the Book of History, Other Earth, the Roush, and *all of it*." He nodded. "Real."

Theo's gaze drifted to the shield above the door. His eyes traced the white band encircling the edge. "Am I back there now? In Other Earth?"

Talya took another step and positioned himself in the center of the room. He scanned the screens. "No, this isn't Other Earth. Though," he paused, "you may see some familiar faces here."

He crossed to the stainless-steel counter and began pushing buttons on its surface. Theo took the opportunity to discreetly pinch his own arm. He winced at the very real pain.

Talya focused on the computer station. "As I said before, this is a game—a game I created for you because, well, as I warned might happen, you've forgotten who you are." Talya pressed one more button, then turned to face him. "And this game might help you remember."

A gold button pulsing with light appeared on each of the dozen or so screens that lined the room, illuminating the words *Start Game*.

Theo's head spun.

"What do you say?" Talya approached him. "Would you like to play the game?"

Images flickered through Theo's mind: a desert wilderness, a lion made of sand, green waters, and a boy with bright blue eyes. But none of the images made sense. They were disjointed and foggy, as if they were memories of a dream.

He eyed Talya skeptically. "How?"

"How? How what?" Talya repeated.

"How do I play?"

The old man's face brightened. He moved with a surprising quickness to the computer station nearest to Theo. "Why it's quite simple. First you must select your avatar."

Theo stepped up to the counter and stared at the screen directly in front of him. The words *Start Game* continued to pulse on the monitor.

Talya cleared his throat.

"Oh." Theo reached forward and tapped his index

finger against the touch screen.

The button disappeared, replaced by an emerald-green background. A characterized image of Theo dressed in a black T-shirt, jeans, and Converse sneakers appeared. The image slowly rotated 360 degrees.

"That's me."

Talya glanced at Theo from the corner of his eye. "Is it now?"

Theo stared at the screen, not registering the question. "This is crazy."

Talya chuckled and patted his shoulder. "Now, before selecting your avatar, you should understand your quest. To win this game, you must rescue the princess and save the Kingdom of Viren." He paused. "Viren—*green* in Latin—a significant detail of course." He continued without further explanation. "As I was saying, you must rescue the princess and save Viren from the dark stranger who has overtaken the kingdom. Additionally, you'll need to find a book. That is the only way to win this game and return to the other game."

"The other game?"

"Mmm. The game of life." Talya nodded. "But the book is of utmost importance. It's the key to your return."

Theo shook his head. Dozens of questions swarmed his mind. "A book? The Book of History? But that went missing a long time ago." A sensory memory overwhelmed Theo—the scents of aged paper and dusty leather. He instinctively touched his right shoulder. "Did you take it from the library? Is it here? How did you get it?"

Talya held up a hand to silence him, watching as Theo slowly lowered his palm from his opposite arm. "I said nothing of a library, only a book."

Theo started to speak, then stopped.

"Save your questions. All will make sense in time." Talya flashed a warm smile. "Now, as I said, we must select your avatar. I will choose the first one for you." He swiped a knobby finger over the screen.

The character's attire changed to a white tunic with billowy sleeves, brown pants tucked into tall leather boots, and a rust-colored vest. An instrument hung from his right shoulder by a bright-red strap. A brown leather satchel slung across the left.

Theo leaned in for a closer look. "Is that a ukelele?"

"A lute," Talya corrected him.

Several icons appeared on the left-hand side of the screen, along with a text box across the bottom. Theo leaned in and read aloud.

"Avatar Backstory: a fourteen-year-old boy, citizen of Viren, whose two parents, Reid and Louisa"—Theo stiffened, then continued—"whose two parents have been taken captive and are being held inside the palace dungeons." He swallowed, then turned to face Talya. "Those are my real parents' names … *Were* my real parents' names." Theo wanted to ask Talya if he'd known, but he couldn't bring himself to ask the question—or hear the answer.

Instead, he turned away from the old man and pointed to the word *bard* at the top of the screen. "What's a bard?"

Talya paused before answering. "A musician and poet, one gifted in lyric, word, and song—an entertainer. These individuals played a key role in passing down stories of great heroes in ancient times."

"A singer? Can't I be something cool, like a warrior?"

"Of course, later, when it is your turn to pick. But for now, trust me, your gift as a bard is strong. You may choose your avatar's name, however. You can make one up or use your own."

Theo frowned, not sure how he felt about Talya selecting the bard and wondering what he meant by "when it is your turn to pick."

"Uh, I guess I'll go with Theo."

Talya tapped the avatar, leaned over the desk, then typed in *Theo*.

His name flashed at the top of the screen.

"Now, with each avatar you play, you'll have a

unique backstory. Your player will be equipped with two pre-selected items"—Talya gestured to the lute and satchel—"and a third item of your choice." He scrolled through the icons on the left-hand side of the screen. Images of a hunting knife, journal, and compass scrolled past. "You'll play three different avatars in this game, and as I said before, later you'll have the chance to make these selections and choices for yourself, but for now" —he tapped the screen—"I suggest you take the water flask."

A canteen-like vessel appeared on Theo's avatar, strapped to his waist with a leather cord. Talya pressed his hands together.

"There, that should do it." He faced Theo. "Now, the next bit I must move through quickly, and again, I must ask you to suspend your questions." He drew a deep breath and continued.

"This building is called a Waystation. There are three inside this game, including this one. When you exit this Waystation, you'll find yourself inside the game with NPCs."

"NPCs? Non-player characters?"

"I see you're familiar with the terminology."

Theo shrugged. "I play games back home."

"Oh good, so these next few rules should feel familiar to you. Yes, NPCs are non-player characters generated by the software of the game. You're distinguished from them by your Life Bars." Talya tapped Theo's right shoulder. "Inside the game, five bars will appear on your arm, indicating how much time you have left before you need to reach the next Waystation to recharge. You'll see your Life Bars fade one by one as time passes *and* as you use your avatar's skills. The more you play a particular avatar, the greater your skill level, but it will come at a great cost. As your skills grow stronger, your Life Bars will fade faster."

"What happens if I run out of time? Do I die?"

"No, but you'll fall unconscious and become stuck in the game."

Theo stiffened. "I'll be stuck in the game for real?"

Talya's right eyebrow rose. "Just make sure you get to a Waystation before your Life Bars run out. As I said, you'll have five. But because two factors deplete them, there is no direct measurement of how much time they provide—somewhere between seven and ten days is a good estimate, but it could be more or much less."

Talya paused to take a breath.

"Other important things to know: Non-player characters cannot see the Waystations. Each time you enter a Waystation, you must select your new avatar before you re-enter the game. And each time you re-enter, your new avatar will be refreshed. All wounds and injures will be healed, and your strength will be renewed."

Theo's mind spun at the overload of information.

Talya tapped his chin. "What else? Oh, yes. I know." He cleared his throat. "Whatever you do in the game will affect the game and become a part of the game's history. So even when you change avatars, the events that happened in your previous avatar will still have happened, but they'll have been done by an NPC. You'll remember those events as if you've always been the new avatar and the events were done by someone else. Make sense?"

"Uh … This doesn't sound like any game I've ever played before …"

Talya waved away Theo's questions before he could ask them. "Don't overthink it. Now, this is the most important part to understand." Talya inched closer and lowered his voice. "Once you enter the game, you'll forget everything I've just told you."

The subtle hum of the Waystation lingered after his words.

Theo stared at him for a long moment, then furrowed his brow.

"*Everything*," Talya said with a twinkle in his eye. "Of course, you're wondering why I just explained all those rules …" He grinned mischievously. "Well, that's what makes it a game, is it not?"

Theo pressed his lips together, not sure how to answer.

Talya pointed to the bare, curved wall where Theo had entered the Waystation. A black door was now visible with a pulsing, gold button that read *Enter Game*. "Once you step through that door, you won't remember that you're in a game. You'll be fully immersed in the world as Theo the bard, not Theo the boy from Florida whose father recently passed."

Talya paused and held Theo's stare, then placed a hand on Theo's shoulder. "I grieve with you, my boy."

Pressure formed behind Theo's eyes. He blinked.

Talya nodded, dropped his hand, then lowered his voice. "I repeat, when you change avatars, you'll remember only the new role you're playing. You'll have no memory of being the bard, but you'll remember the feelings of being the bard. For example, should you develop a bond with someone, or fear of another, you'll retain that trust and fear as your new avatar, though you won't know why. The details will be foggy as if in a dream."

"*This* feels like a dream," Theo mumbled. His mind swirled with all the rules and information Talya had given him—the information he'd soon forget. He sighed. "Can I ask one question?"

Talya gripped his staff with both hands and leaned forward. "I do believe I'm finished with my instructions. Ask away."

Theo chewed the inside of his lip, then said, "So everything that happened before in Other Earth … It was real? You're sure?"

The skin around Talya's eyes crinkled with his smile. "As real as everything else. Yes, everything that happened to you in Other Earth is real. But just as you'll soon forget your life in Florida—and my longwinded instructions here in this Waystation—so also will you forget that Other Earth was real." His eyebrows darted up. "You'll even forget that *you* are real."

Theo tilted his head. "But how can I win the game if I don't remember who I am?"

Talya tapped his staff against the floor. "Precisely, my friend! Your journey here is to remember who you really are, beyond here and beyond your life in Florida." His eyes gleamed with mystery. He pointed to the black door. "It's time."

He placed a hand on Theo's arm and led him toward the exit. "As for your Life Bars, once inside the game, you'll remember that you have them—because you can see them—but you won't understand their true meaning."

"What do you mean?"

"You'll assume the dark stranger who invaded Viren has cursed you—though, I must say, he doesn't actually have that kind of power. When you, as your avatar, see your Life Bars diminish, you'll know that you need to get to a Waystation. Their locations are a part of your programming."

Theo stared at the black door and the glowing button before turning back to face Talya. His eyes drifted over the man's shoulder to the mysterious white door on the other side of the room and the shield above it. "What's in that room?"

"That," Talya said, "is the charging station. You don't need it now, but you will once your Life Bars run out." He placed his hands on Theo's shoulders and spun him back around to face the door. "Remember your objectives in this game: save the princess and the Kingdom of Viren, and find the book." He squeezed Theo's shoulders and released them. "When you enter the game, you'll pick up where you left off—being chased."

"Chased?" Theo had completely forgotten about the archer and his comrades.

"Yes," Talya said with a smile in his voice. "*Chased.* Good luck, Theo. You won't see me again until you discover your true purpose."

"True purpose?" Theo turned. "You didn't say anything about—"

Talya was gone.

An unsettling feeling washed over Theo. He shook off a shiver and faced the black door again. Lifting his hand, he hesitated and considered Talya's words.

Other Earth was real.

But he'd forgotten.

Distant memories of that world tickled his mind, then vanished.

You have forgotten who you are. And this game might help you remember.

Memories of his father fought for his attention. Theo touched his chest, realizing that if he played this game, soon he'd even forget his dad.

But he'd remember again—when he won the game.

If he won.

Talya's warning about becoming stuck in the game worried him.

Theo shook his head. "It's just a game," he said to himself, then tapped his finger against the button.

The glowing words disappeared, replaced by the blinking numbers three … two … one …

The soft hum of the Waystation intensified.

The floor vibrated beneath Theo's feet.

And then the Waystation was gone.

Chapter Four

A SOFT BREEZE RUSTLED Theo's hair. Sunlight warmed his skin. He blinked against the daylight and spun in a slow circle, taking in his surroundings. He stood in the same circular clearing where he'd found the Waystation, but the building had vanished.

He glanced down at his body, noticing for the first time that he now wore the attire of the bard.

Remembering what Talya had said, he pushed up the billowy white sleeve on his right arm. Five black bars marked his skin like a tattoo, one stacked on top of the other.

"Cool," he whispered. "I really am in a game." Then he stopped. "I thought Talya said I wouldn't remember …"

But not only did Theo remember everything the old man had said to him inside the Waystation, he remembered his life in Florida *and* his avatar's backstory as if it were his own history.

He reached for the lute strapped to his shoulder and examined the artistry, recalling the moment his mother—or rather, his avatar's mother—had given the stringed instrument to him as a gift. She'd always encouraged him in his musical talents.

Theo laughed. "This is amazing!"

He adjusted the lute on his shoulder, then started across the field, wondering why Talya had said he'd forget when he clearly remembered.

"Okay," he said to himself while pushing through the tall grasses, "my goal is to rescue the princess, save the Kingdom of Viren, and find a book. Easy enough." He swallowed. "Rescue princess," he repeated, "save Viren, and find …" He paused. "And find … Well, I just need to worry about Viren and the princess, and then …" Theo froze near the edge of the clearing where the field gave way to trees. He scratched his head. "I need to save Viren, and I'll do that by finding …"

His thoughts blurred, then vanished. "What was I saying?" He scanned the grass and forest and shook his head, blinking several times. A subtle ache pulsed at his temples. He felt disoriented for a moment, as if he were about to fall over, and then the sensation passed. Theo stood upright. His mind cleared and his thoughts returned to his current focus—running for his life.

"I have to get out of here," he mumbled, still feeling

the adrenaline coursing through his veins as he recalled the arrows whizzing past his head.

Two days ago, Dark Riders had taken his parents captive. He crouched low, wondering if they could have tracked him this far. Creeping quietly, Theo made his way through the remaining few feet of tall grass to the tree line, hoping the archer and his comrades had given up their search.

A twig snapped underfoot.

"Hold it right there."

Theo slowly turned to his right, hands held up in a sign of surrender. A man dressed in a hooded cloak rose from his crouched position, bow drawn. At less than five yards away, Theo knew, this time, the archer wouldn't miss.

The man whistled.

The sound of horses' hooves rumbled in the distance, growing louder with every second. In mere moments, two riders joined them, dressed in forest-green cloaks that matched the archer in front of him.

They dismounted and approached, one of them drawing back his hood, revealing dark-brown skin, a shaven head, and a thick beard. The other unveiled his clean-shaven, fair face and blond hair.

The man with the shaven head spoke first. "Who are you?"

Theo's eyes darted back and forth among the three of them, then landed on the archer. The man questioning him noticed.

"Lower your bow, Elijah. He can't escape us now."

Theo swallowed, watching as the archer lowered his bow but kept it at the ready.

"Now, let's try this again. Who are you?"

Theo wet his lips before speaking. "My name is Theo."

The man stepped closer but spoke to the archer called Elijah. "Where was he?"

Elijah drew back his hood revealing tan skin, dark eyes, and matching dark hair and beard. "Coming out of the clearing."

"I thought you checked the clearing."

"I did. It's as if he vanished for a minute."

"Vanished?" The blond-haired man chuckled. "It seems a teenage bard outwitted you. Clearly you missed him."

"That's enough, Liam," the leader said to him. "He must have hidden himself."

"I checked the entire—"

"Enough." The leader narrowed his eyes at Theo. "Now, tell me, why did you run from us?"

"Because he was shooting arrows at me." Theo pointed to Elijah.

"We shoot at any threat." Elijah looked him up and down. "Are you a spy for the Dark Riders?"

Fury flared in Theo's gut. He turned his head to the side and spat. "How dare you think I'd be associated with them. They imprisoned my family!" He sucked in a sharp breath through his nostrils. "Are *you* with the Dark Riders?"

The leader exchanged glances with his two men. He didn't answer. "Where are you from?"

Theo hesitated, not sure if he could trust these men. "Viren," he said.

"Who are your parents? And more importantly, why were they taken captive?"

Theo chewed the inside of his lip, debating how much he should share.

Seeing his hesitation, the leader said, "We're not with the Dark Riders. Your story is safe with us."

Theo eyed them suspiciously, recalling the rumors he'd heard about a rebel group who'd escaped the city.

"When my father saw the Dark Riders coming, he hid me under the floorboards." Theo looked at the ground. "There wasn't enough room for my mother." Clearing his throat, he continued. "My father's name is Reid Dunning. He's a professor at the university. Three days ago, he spoke out against the king in one of his lectures. Word travels fast in the city now. The next day, a pair of Dark Riders carried him off, along with my mother."

Theo's mind replayed the memory: the terror on his mother's face, the pounding of men breaking down the door, the sound of his father's voice whispering, "Stay invisible," as he sealed Theo under the floor.

Theo had hidden there for hours, waiting for the cover of darkness, before packing a small bag and escaping the city with nothing more than his life and lute. Pressure formed behind his eyes as he thought of his last moments with his parents.

The one called Liam stepped forward. "You're Reid's boy?"

"You know my father?"

"He's one of the finest educators in all of Viren. I'm sorry to hear of his capture."

The leader exchanged glances with Liam, then turned to Theo. "So you escaped. What is your plan then? Where are you headed?"

Theo swallowed. "You wouldn't know anything about the rebellion, would you?"

The leader didn't flinch. "What do you know of the rebellion?"

Theo dared to step toward him. "Only rumors I've heard in the city: that the future prince of Viren, William, fled the kingdom and escaped the Dark Riders, taking a handful of the King's Guard with him." He paused dramatically. "And that some believe William will be their salvation and return to the city to liberate it."

The leader said nothing, but out of the corner of Theo's eye, he saw Liam smirk. "Sounds like we're quite famous."

Elijah shot Liam a glare.

"What? It's obvious the bard knows who we are. Perhaps he's even written a song about us? If not, he should."

The leader held up his hand, and the other two fell silent. Before he could speak, Theo said, "Take me with you!"

Elijah scoffed.

"Please!" Theo begged. "I have nowhere to go."

The leader stared at him a little too long.

"Conrad, you can't seriously be entertaining this," Elijah protested. "He could still be a spy."

"He's just a boy," Liam said. "And I knew his father." He gestured to Theo. "He even looks like him."

The leader, Conrad, folded his arms over his chest.

"Look," Theo said, speaking quickly. "I can see you're conflicted—"

"We're not conflicted." Elijah interrupted.

Theo didn't stop. "But I could be of great use to the rebellion."

"How?" Conrad asked. "Are you a warrior?"

"No."

"A healer?"

"No."

"Intelligent?"

"Not particularly."

Conrad shook his head. "Then what good are you to us?"

Theo shifted on his feet. "Well, I have a way with words." He thought for a moment. "And my mother says I have the voice of an angel."

Elijah rolled his eyes.

"Let me show you," Theo insisted, swinging his lute forward and strumming a chord.

The three rebels stood still but didn't protest.

Lifting his chin, Theo sang along with the tune.

"The sun shines bright over Viren;
Though the darkness clouds her eyes.
But the Prince will come and clear the mist;
That blinds the old king's sight."

Conrad's face softened, then Elijah's, as Theo continued the song which he made up as he went.

By the time Theo had finished, Liam was grinning.

Theo strummed the last chord and held the final note a beat longer than normal, then returned the lute to his shoulder. "Well?"

"Looks like your mother was right," Liam said.

A smile formed on Theo's face.

Liam looked toward Conrad. "I do miss the music of Viren. Are we not allowed to have simple pleasures even though we are on the run for our lives?"

Conrad shrugged.

Liam turned to Elijah. "What do you say?"

"Fine." Elijah relaxed his posture. "He's quite skilled, but he's still the most annoying boy I've ever met."

Stars glimmered overhead, making their first appearance of the night. Theo rode behind Liam on his horse. He shifted uncomfortably. They'd been traveling the entire day through the thick forests that lay to the west of Viren. Thankfully, they were getting close to the rebel camp, or at least that's what Liam had said about a mile back.

The sound of rushing water reached Theo's ears from somewhere up ahead.

In front of them, Conrad pulled his horse to a stop and dismounted. Liam followed suit, offering Theo a hand down from the horse. Behind them, Elijah did the same. The men led the horses by their reins on foot for several yards until a stream became visible. They followed it for another several paces until they reached a small waterfall.

"Welcome to camp," Liam said.

Theo glanced around the untouched forest. "Where is it?"

Liam smirked, then nodded his head in the direction of the waterfall, where Conrad was leading his horse behind the thick flow into a barely visible crevice in the rock.

Theo followed Liam with Elijah close behind.

The pound of the waterfall was deafening as they approached. Mist dampened Theo's skin, but his clothes remained dry as he navigated around the waterfall's stream. Once behind the curtain of water, the cavern opened up. Conrad whistled, and another whistle replied from somewhere in the darkness of the grotto.

Theo blindly followed the rebel men into the hollow stone and around a bend. Another crevice led deeper into the rock, wide enough only for them to lead their horses through single file. Warm light flickered ahead, and after a few yards, the crevice opened into a vast cave. Theo blinked and took in the scene.

A fire sat in the center beneath a vaulted ceiling adorned with stalactites, where smoke vented through a narrow fissure in the stone. Three men sat around the fire. A woman perched on a log across from them, slicing root vegetables into a pot of boiling water. Dimly lit bales of hay lined the left side of the stone perimeter, where a dozen or so horses nibbled from the stacks. Water streamed down the stone on the back wall, filling the echoey chamber with the soothing sound of running water. It bubbled into a small pool where a couple of children filled clay vessels, presumably for cooking and drinking. The right side of the cave appeared to be the sleeping quarters. Several pallets lined the ground, stacked with blankets. There were even a couple of tents.

A man appeared beside Liam and took the horses. Conrad thanked him, then lifted a hand in greeting to the men by the campfire. The one in the center caught his attention and stood. The other two quickly dispersed.

Conrad motioned for Liam, Elijah, and Theo to follow.

When they neared the man, Theo froze. Firelight highlighted his strong jaw and illuminated his sandy blond hair and hazel eyes.

"You're the prince," Theo said without thinking.

"Soon-to-be prince," Conrad said, reaching out a hand to the man who was clearly Sir William Atwood. The knight returned Conrad's greeting, clasping a hand around his forearm, but his fair eyes didn't leave Theo's.

"Who's this?" William asked.

"His name is Theo Dunning," Conrad explained.

"Son of Reid Dunning."

"Reid Dunning?" William exchanged glances with Conrad. "He's one of the finest professors I had during my time at the university."

"That's what I said," Liam chimed in.

"Why's he with you?" William asked.

"We'll fill you in." Conrad motioned to the woman slicing vegetables. "Eloise, can you please show Theo around, maybe find him some clothes?"

"Of course." The woman wiped her hands on her apron, then grabbed Theo by the arm. "Come with me, young man."

Theo looked over his shoulder as he followed her, watching William, Conrad, Liam, and Elijah take a seat around the fire. Eloise led him to one of the tents. She ducked in and returned a minute later with a folded blanket and a change of clothes.

"Here you are. You may change inside the tent. Then just find yourself a pallet for the night. We'll be serving the evening meal a little later."

Theo nodded. "Thanks." He ducked into the tent and waited a few seconds, watching her silhouette disappear outside the small canvas structure. When he peeked his head out, she was gone.

Clutching the blanket and change of clothes to his chest, Theo snuck around the dimly lit perimeter of the cave, passing a few small children playing a game with carved dice. They watched him but said nothing. He passed the sleeping area, tossing the blanket and clothes onto one of the pallets, then made his way to the streaming water centered on the back wall. Dipping his hands into the pool, he cupped a quick drink to his lips, then splashed his face. He stared up at the spot where the stream of water entered the rock, guessing it came from the same source as the waterfall.

Casting a quick glance to the left and right, Theo snuck toward the center of the cave, using the sounds of bubbling water to mask his footsteps. A makeshift kitchen area sat between him and the fire. Men and women bustled about, chopping and mixing. He crept through the shadows until he reached a stack of several large packs of grain, situated several feet back from the fire. He positioned himself behind it, then leaned forward to listen.

"So there's still no news of Rosaline?" William asked.

Conrad shifted beside him. "No, my friend. I wish I had something good to report."

William sighed. "I should have gone with you. What good am I to Rosaline if I'm stuck here in this cave?" He tossed up a hand.

"We've been over this," Conrad said. "The Dark Riders are after you. *You* are their target. And we need you alive." He paused. "You're the only hope of Viren."

William scoffed.

"Plus we're rather fond of you," Liam added.

That produced a slight chuckle from William.

"We can't allow you to die," Conrad continued. "You're Rosaline's betrothed, the future prince—and one day, king—of Viren. If you perish, she'll be available to marry another." Conrad lowered his voice. "You know this is what the dark stranger desires."

William shifted. "I know all these things, but I feel powerless here. As you said, this is my future kingdom. Which means this is *my* battle."

Conrad shook his head. "This is *our* battle."

William nodded. "Thank you." He paused for a long moment. "And what of the king? Any word?"

"You mean the king who betrayed us all?" Elijah asked.

"He hasn't betrayed us," Conrad said. "We're the King's Guard. He'd never turn against his people willingly. He's bewitched, and his actions aren't his own. The new laws and mandates, even the formation of the Dark Riders, have been influenced by that mysterious stranger."

"Agreed," William said. "King Tyrus is not in his right mind. Now, tell me: was your mission successful?"

"We've located the construction site of the new

outpost," Liam said. "During the day, it's bustling with builders, but at night, only three Dark Riders guard it. If we attack under the cover of darkness, we should easily neutralize them with four of our best men."

William nodded. "Very well. We must move quickly then. We need information about the state of the kingdom. It's been two weeks, and we don't know what's taking place inside our own city walls." He glanced at Conrad. "That boy you found … You said he recently fled the city?"

Theo shifted behind the sacks of grain.

"Surely he could fill us in on the state of affairs."

Conrad started to stand. "I can fetch him."

Theo stepped forward and into the firelight. "I can tell you about the city."

Elijah tossed up his hands. "See! The most obnoxious boy ever."

Liam chuckled. "And a spy, as it turns out."

Elijah shook his head, watching Theo take a seat on the log beside Liam. He removed his satchel and lute from his shoulders and placed them on the ground at his feet.

"Well then, Bard," William said. "Tell us. What's it like inside our city's walls?"

Theo leaned forward. "It's worse than you can imagine: weekly raids on homes, nightly curfews, higher taxes, rations, and anyone who speaks out against King Tyrus, the Dark Riders, or Marsuuv is thrown into prison."

"Marsuuv?" William asked.

Theo nodded. "The dark stranger." He touched the sleeve of his shirt, feeling his warm skin beneath the billowing fabric, knowing the markings that lay there—the curse of Marsuuv.

"And the princess?" William asked, interrupting his thoughts.

"No one has seen her since Marsuuv arrived. My father believes she's being held captive."

"Of course she is," William said emphatically. "And the king?"

Theo paused before continuing. "The king stopped making appearances a week ago. Marsuuv and the Dark Riders have taken over, and their numbers have tripled. There are at least fifty now. They stay in the shadows, but I've heard stories of them."

His mind drifted back to hiding under the floorboards of his own home, listening to his father's protests and mother's screams as the dark hooded men—men who used to be among the King's Guard—dragged them from their home. They were loyal to a fault, even when their king descended into darkness. Theo locked eyes with William. "Even the civilians have been told to shoot the rebels on sight if they see you."

Conrad straightened. "It's worse than we imagined."

"Indeed," Theo said. "Our once beautiful Viren has dimmed from shades of emerald and chartreuse to a murky, mucky olive."

Liam cocked an eyebrow at him. "Odd choice of words, Bard."

Theo shrugged. "She has darkened, mimicking the man who has enslaved her, Marsuuv—truly a man of shadows." He paused when he said it, the description stirring something familiar inside him. "A man of shadows," he repeated. "A true adversary."

"But how can such an adversary appear from nowhere?" Elijah asked. "Do the people of the city still not know where he's from?"

"What does it matter where he's from?" William asked. "His intentions are clear. He wants to marry the princess and inherit the kingdom."

"Impossible," Conrad said. "She's betrothed to you."

"Can't he simply marry her?" Theo asked.

"Oh the ignorance of the young," Liam said, placing a hand on Theo's shoulder. "You know nothing of the customs of love."

Elijah shook his head. "The youth have little respect for our customs—or anything else. A betrothed man or woman can't marry another unless their suitor renounces their engagement or dies."

"That's why the king wants you dead?" Theo said, looking at William.

"Keep up, Bard, it's not complicated." Elijah snickered.

"It's fine, Elijah," William said, holding up a hand. "Days after the dark stranger—Marsuuv, you called him?"

Theo nodded.

"After he arrived, I learned the king had ordered my execution because he wanted to betroth Rosaline to another. I can only assume it's to this Marsuuv. I fled the city to protect my life and my union to her."

"And he didn't flee alone," Conrad said. "Thirty-seven of us managed to escape: nineteen of us former King's Guard; the rest, loyal civilians to the true king. We've been on the run for two weeks. A few days into hiding, we stumbled upon this cave system and have been here ever since."

Theo glanced at Elijah before shifting his attention to William. "The Dark Riders have imprisoned by parents, and you, Sir William, are truly the only hope of Viren. As the princess's betrothed, you're the rightful inheritor of the kingdom. Only you can liberate us." He dipped his head. "It is my honor to serve you"—he paused—"my future king."

Liam chuckled. "A way with words, indeed."

Theo ignored him. "I want to come with you when you go to the outpost."

Elijah snorted a laugh. "You're a simple bard. Our mission isn't your concern."

Theo jumped to his feet. "I won't sit back while my parents are in prison!" A wave of grief washed over him, the pain as fresh as if he'd already lost them. "I told you I can be helpful. Take me with you."

"No offense, Bard, but what do you plan to do? Soothe the Dark Riders to sleep with your lullabies?" Liam elbowed him with a chuckle.

Heat flushed Theo's cheeks.

"Enough," William said, standing. "Our plan is set. I'm certain you'll be a valuable member to our group, but you're just a boy—and a bard—and you won't be coming on this mission." He gestured around the cavern. "Make yourself useful here." To the three men, he said, "Ready yourselves. We leave before dawn."

William clapped a hand on Theo's shoulder before leaving. "It's good to have you among us, Bard. Welcome to the rebellion."

Chapter Five

THEO URGED HIS HORSE FORWARD, trying to choose the quietest path through the forest. Morning light angled through the trees and warmed his skin. Several hours had passed since he'd snuck away from the rebel camp, leaving just before dawn with one of their horses. He'd waited until William and his three men had left for the outpost, then followed at a distance so as not to be detected.

He'd last seen a sign of the rebel warriors at least a mile ago, and he was beginning to feel uncertain about his navigation skills. Last night he'd overheard Conrad tell William the outpost was due east of the caves, near the outskirts of the farmlands. But if that was true, it would be about a day's ride from the rebel camp. That left far too much opportunity for Theo to get lost.

He adjusted his lute and satchel, pausing as his fingers grazed the shoulder of his right arm. He considered lifting his sleeve, then dropped his hand, not daring to reveal the five black bars that marked him as cursed.

Theo gripped the reins tighter, remembering the moment he'd discovered the strange markings after his parents were arrested. He'd first noticed them the night he fled the city when a searing heat burned across his flesh. He'd yanked up his sleeve, revealing five black tattoolike marks. In that moment, Theo knew he'd been cursed by Marsuuv, the same man who was responsible for the imprisonment of his parents. But what Theo didn't understand was *how* he knew this—which made the curse even more unsettling.

He recalled the way he'd traced a finger over each of the five bars, his mind coming alive with a sudden knowing. Marsuuv had marked Theo because his father had spoken out against the king, and now, Theo would also pay for his father's actions.

As a result of this curse, his days were numbered.

Once again, Theo didn't understand how he knew this. He just did.

A loud rushing sound erupted through the trees to the right. Theo's horse spooked and reared up, nearly knocking him off its back. He grasped the reins and squeezed his thighs tighter against the muscled animal, certain he was about to witness a Dark Rider burst through the forest.

But it was Conrad who charged him on horseback, sword drawn.

"You?" Conrad demanded. "What are you doing here? I nearly killed you!"

Theo's horse snorted but returned her front feet to the ground. She stomped as Theo patted her neck while trying to catch his breath.

Conrad whistled, and William, Elijah, and Liam appeared on their horses.

Elijah groaned. "The bard?"

"We thought you were a Dark Rider following us," Liam said.

William folded his arms across his chest but looked amused. "You're awfully bold for a bard."

"I believe you mean *annoying*." Elijah glared.

Liam grinned. "At least he's entertaining."

"This is your fault." Elijah jabbed a finger at Liam. "You said you knew his father and that his music would do us some good. So far, the bard is nothing but trouble."

William maneuvered his horse between Conrad and Theo. "Ride him back to camp."

"Respectfully, my lord, we can't." Conrad sheathed his sword. "If we turn around now, we'll never make it to the outpost by nightfall. And, we'll need all four of us to apprehend the Dark Riders."

"Then send him back alone," Elijah interjected. "He made it this far by himself, surely he can find his way back."

William eyed Theo. "No. He's not exactly stealthy. If we heard him following us, so would anyone else in the forest. We can't risk him leading someone back to our camp." William snapped his reins and continued forward. "He comes with us."

Conrad exchanged glances with Elijah, then shook his head and joined William.

Before following, Elijah cut his eyes at Theo and said, "Stay close and be quiet. If you die, it's your own fault." His horse trotted after Conrad's.

Liam pulled up beside Theo and shrugged, then motioned for Theo to go first. "After you, Bard. Looks like you may get to lull the Dark Riders to sleep after all."

Theo urged his horse forward, grateful they were allowing him to come but wondering if he'd regret joining them.

They reached the outpost by nightfall, hiding in the thick of the trees until the sun had completely descended. The darkness of the forest nearly camouflaged William and his men as they tied their horses to trees.

"I still think we should tie him up with the horses," Elijah whispered, nodding in Theo's direction.

William shook his head. "It's clear that if we leave him behind, he'll try to follow us anyway. At least now, we can make sure he stays quiet."

Elijah pulled his rope tight around the tree, then secured a knot. "Be silent," he whispered to Theo. "And stay out of our way."

Liam popped in between them, "Just stay invisible," he said in a teasing whisper.

His words struck Theo.

Stay invisible.

The final words his father had spoken as he concealed Theo beneath the floorboards of their home. The last thing Theo had heard from his parents.

A fresh wave of grief washed over him.

The words stirred something deeper, but Theo didn't have time to place it. William and his men were on the move, creeping through the edge of the forest toward the fields.

As they slinked closer, a small bonfire became visible in the distance. Three silhouettes sat around it. Theo's stomach flipped. He'd never seen a Dark Rider, but the memories of their violent shouts filled his mind. Theo winced at the memory of his mother's cries followed by a silencing blow. Feelings of rage and grief mingled inside him and swelled. He swallowed the emotions and fixed his eyes on a half-completed watchtower that loomed in the dim moonlight.

"Is that the outpost?" Theo asked before thinking.

Elijah elbowed him.

Theo pressed his lips together and followed across the field, not daring to speak another word.

About ten yards away, William held up a fist. The other three rebels froze. Theo did the same, watching as one of the Dark Riders stood from his place by the fire, then wandered off to the right.

William nodded at Elijah, then motioned for him to follow the man.

Elijah silently slipped away.

William pointed at Theo next, jabbed a finger at the ground, then pressed it to his lips.

The message was clear.

Theo nodded and crouched low, watching as William gave hand signals to Conrad and Liam. The three of them crept toward the bonfire, dividing into a formation of three. Once they were closer to the firelight, Theo couldn't make out the details, but sounds of a scuffle reached his ears. Silhouettes blurred against the blaze, and in mere moments it was over.

One of the rebels whistled, and Elijah appeared from the left, dragging a bound and unconscious man.

Theo took this as his signal to rejoin them.

When he reached the bonfire, William, Conrad, and Liam had also bound the other two guards, but only one remained conscious. His eyes flickered to Theo as he approached.

Theo couldn't help but wonder if this man had played a part in his parents' arrest.

William hovered over him. "I'm shocked, Henry," he said to the man. "You and I trained together as boys. You were a loyal member of the King's Guard. Look at you now."

"Look at me?" The Dark Rider glared at William. "You're the one who's rebelled against the king." He spat on William's boot.

The prince remained unfazed. "You know that isn't our king. The man on the throne may be Tyrus, but he's not in his right mind." Intensity creased William's face. "Now, tell me what you know of this Marsuuv. What has he done to the king, and where is he keeping the princess?"

The Dark Rider stared; his jaw muscles tensed.

Pressure formed in Theo's gut, pushing upward against his diaphragm. The tension rose, expanding in his throat with an unsettling force.

"Well?" Conrad demanded while staring at the Dark Rider. "Are you going to answer the prince or not?"

Theo's insides tingled.

Conrad drew a dagger. "Do you need some encouragement? I'd be happy to help." He knelt beside the bound man.

A subtle buzz raced up Theo's arms and stirred his mind. Before he could stop himself, he stepped forward into the firelight and blurted, "Did the dark stranger curse the king?"

The four rebels turned and stared.

The Dark Rider watched Theo with curious eyes.

"Not now, Bard," Elijah snapped. "Get back."

Theo ignored him, feeling the tingle in his gut, as if it were propelling his words. "Just be plain with me. Did he curse him?" Theo stepped beside William and stared down at the bound Dark Rider.

Elijah grabbed Theo by the arm and yanked. "Why on earth do you think this man would speak to you? I thought I told you to—"

"*Cursed*," the Dark Rider repeated. "An interesting choice of word."

William motioned for Elijah to release Theo's arm. The future prince watched the interaction with interest.

Theo asked the question again boldly. "You have nothing to lose in speaking the truth here. Speak plainly. Did Marsuuv curse King Tyrus or did he not?"

The Dark Rider paused for a long moment, his eyes never leaving Theo's. Eventually he blinked, then said,

"I believe the word you're looking for is *poison*."

William shifted beside Theo.

The Dark Rider spoke in a slow, deliberate tone. "The king has been poisoned—his eyes and mind clouded." He paused for a long moment, then snapped his head as if awakening from a trance. After blinking several times, he looked away. "I know nothing of the princess."

William cast a sideways glance at Theo, then yanked the Dark Rider to his feet.

"We should kill him," Elijah said. "All three of them."

"No," William said in a calm and commanding voice. "Bloodshed isn't necessary."

Bubbling laughter erupted from the Dark Rider. "And that is why you'll lose. Because you're a weak fool!"

His laughter ceased abruptly, cut short by the sound of Conrad's fist thumping the man's skull. The man slumped, unconscious.

William glared at Conrad.

"What?" Conrad said. "He's not bleeding."

William shook his head. "Drag them into the field and bind them together so they can't escape. We must leave quickly."

William stooped to grab the Dark Rider under the arms while Conrad hoisted his legs. The prince shuffled backward into the field, eyes never leaving Theo's.

Theo rode in the middle of the group, Conrad ahead of him with William in the lead, while Elijah and Liam guarded the rear. They'd fled immediately after their encounter with the Dark Riders and rode all night and into the next day. The warm afternoon sun lulled Theo into a sleepy state. He shifted to stay awake, wondering how much farther they had to travel before reaching camp. The familiar landscape suggested they were getting close.

Ahead of them, William slowed, allowing Conrad to take the lead while he sidled up next to Theo. "I haven't thanked you yet."

"Thanked me?" Theo asked.

William nodded but stared straight ahead. "For acquiring a critical piece of information."

"You mean about the poison?"

William turned to face him. "How did you know what to ask him? How did you—a bard—manage to pry such crucial information from a former King's Guard? And with such little effort? It's as if he wanted to tell you."

Theo thought for a moment before speaking, ignoring the subtle itch of the bars on his shoulder. He considered the tingling buzz that had filled his gut the night before. It had bubbled upward, as if propelling his words. Theo shrugged. "My mother says that I have a way with words. I suppose I just asked the right question in the right way."

William watched him for a moment, then said, "I wonder what kind of poison could do such a thing to our king."

Ahead of them, Conrad jerked his horse to a stop and drew his sword. Liam and Elijah immediately raced past Theo and William with weapons drawn. William snapped his horse's reins and rode forward to meet them. Theo followed close behind, craning his neck to see around the rebels.

Conrad maneuvered his horse in front of William's. The other two flanked the sides, ensuring their future prince's protection.

"Who are you? Conrad demanded, sword pointed downward at a threat Theo couldn't see. "And what are you doing here?"

Theo nudged his horse forward and peered between the rebels' shoulders to get a better look.

A girl about his age stood in the center of the trail, dressed in a well-worn tunic and pants, brown hair tied back in a braid, and hands held up in surrender.

"Please," she said. "I mean you no harm." She lowered her hands, then said, "I need your help."

Chapter Six

THEO WATCHED THE GIRL empty her pockets, placing a hunting knife on the ground along with the small leather pouch she wore at her waist. She held up her hands again and turned in a slow circle.

"See? I'm safe. I only want to talk." She completed the circle and stared at Conrad, eyes flickering to Theo for only a moment.

William pushed past Conrad. "Lower your weapons."

Conrad hesitated, then lowered his sword. He didn't sheath it.

"Who are you?" William asked. "And what's a girl your age doing out here alone?"

Theo saw a flash of offense cross her face. "My name is Leah, and I live here in the forest—not alone," she added. "With my parents, which is why I need your help. They've gone missing."

William exchanged a glance with Conrad. "Who are your parents?" the prince asked. "Is your family from Viren?"

"We lived in the city many years ago, but my father moved us out here when I was four. My parents still make trips to the city, though, once every few months for supplies. They left for a supply run two weeks ago, and I haven't seen them since. The entire trip normally takes six days. Please, I need your help. They've been gone too long. I fear something has happened to them."

Theo's stomach dropped. He saw the genuine fear on the girl's face and empathized with her loss.

"This is foolish," Elijah said. "She could be a spy." He turned and glared at Theo. "What are the odds of running into two needy teens in the span of a few days?"

"Pretty good odds considering what's taking place inside the city," Liam interjected.

"What's happening in the city?" the girl asked. "Are my parents in danger?"

William dismounted his horse. "You don't know?"

"Know what?" Her eyes shifted from William's to Theo's, then back.

"A little over a month ago, a dark stranger entered the city seeking audience with King Tyrus. Since his arrival, the princess has vanished, and our kind king has been poisoned, turning him into a tyrant. Our kingdom has become a city of darkness."

The girl flinched. "Poisoned?"

"That's what the Dark Rider told us," Theo said.

Elijah shot him a look. "Quiet, Bard."

"Dark Rider?" she asked, shaking her head. "I'm not familiar with the term."

"Men who formerly served as the King's Guard," William explained, "and who've loyally followed the king into his descent."

"They're hunting William," Theo added.

Elijah jerked his head at Theo. "I said that's enough from you!"

William held up a hand. "It's okay."

"William …" the girl repeated. Recognition dawned on her face. "Sir William Atwood? The future prince of Viren?"

A smile formed on William's face.

Elijah tossed up his hands. "Do we just reveal our identities to anyone now?"

"She's just a girl," Liam said.

Leah thrust a hand onto her hip. "Would *just a girl* know that you and your men have been staying in the caves?"

Theo saw Conrad's knuckles whiten, his fingers clenching the hilt of his sword.

"And," Leah continued, "that you have twenty-one

horses, nineteen men, seven women, and exactly eleven children among you?"

Conrad lifted his sword.

Elijah aimed his bow. "You see! She's a spy."

William motioned for them to lower their weapons once again.

The girl chuckled. "I'm no spy, but I make it my business to know who's invaded the forests surrounding my home."

Theo smirked.

"Wipe that smug look off your face, Bard," Elijah growled.

Theo shrugged, but he couldn't take his eyes off the girl.

"So how do you know so much about our little group?" William asked. "And yet, you know so little of the city."

The girl softened her posture. "As I said, my parents and I moved out here when I was four. I only know the stories they and the few people I've met in their wanderings have shared."

"Did you not make trips to the city with them?"

"No. My mother and I always stayed back. But now that I'm older, I keep watch over the house by myself. Which I'm quite capable of doing," she added. "But shortly after my parents left this last time, a group of thirty-seven strangers showed up in my woods. You must understand, after having seen so few other humans besides my parents for ten years, I was intrigued. Did I spy on your group?" She paused. "Yes. But in my defense, your women speak loudly while collecting berries."

Theo saw Elijah shift.

"After hearing your women describe the city as *unsafe*, I began to worry for my parents. The longer their return delayed, the more concerned I became. Now I feel certain something has happened to them, which is why I approached you. I need your help."

"Don't you fear us?" William asked.

She smiled. "I've been watching long enough to know you're decent. Though, I must say, I didn't realize you're the prince."

Elijah shook his head.

She cleared her throat. "So now, if I may, I'd like to ask a few questions of my own."

William nodded. "Go on."

"Who are these others among you?" Her eyes scanned the three rebels, then landed on Theo.

"These three were part of the Kings Guard." William gestured to his men. "We have other warriors in our group as well, along with the wives and children of a few. We remain loyal to the *true* King Tyrus, not the man who's been poisoned."

Theo saw her shift her weight, then lift her chin. "And the boy?" she asked.

"Him? A bard who's recently joined our troop. Apparently he has a way with words."

"And the voice of an angel," Liam added with a chuckle.

She smiled at Theo, dipped her head, then returned her attention to William. "I must ask you: do you know what may have happened to my parents?"

This time, William shifted. "Young lady, based on what you've shared, I'm afraid your parents may have been taken captive by the Dark Riders."

Her eyes darted to the ground before glancing up at William. "And you're against these Dark Riders? And the stranger who's poisoned the king?"

"Marsuuv," Theo said.

She glanced at him. "Marsuuv?" A bitter look formed on her face as she said the name. "And you wish to overthrow him?"

"I wish to return my true king to the throne and to liberate my beloved city. But most of all, I wish to find my betrothed, Rosaline. No one has seen or heard from her since this Marsuuv arrived."

The girl nodded, a faraway look in her eyes. She pressed her lips together, then said, "Surely you must know the pain I feel at the disappearance of my parents."

Theo found himself nodding, though she'd directed the question at William.

"I surely do."

"Will you help me find them?"

William softened at her request. "Young lady, we seek to liberate all of Viren, and I do hope that means your parents as well, but I can't help you in the way I believe you're asking. We must stay focused on our mission."

Her lips twitched. "And what if I could help you with that mission?"

Elijah scoffed, but William tilted his head.

"My father was—*is* an herbalist," she said.

Conrad interjected. "We already have men and women among us who know how to make tinctures and salves."

She flicked her eyes to him and continued. "My father has many specialties as an herbalist, and one of his particular fascinations is poisons."

William straightened. "Interesting."

"Yes," the girl said, nodding her head and smiling. "Interesting. He might be exactly what you need."

William paused, then asked, "Did your father ever speak of a poison that clouds the mind and eyes?"

The girl stiffened. Her smile faded.

"No?" William asked. "You've never heard of it?"

The girl caught Theo's attention once again. "Actually, yes. He did tell me of a poison like the one you describe. In fact, it poisoned *him*."

Theo leaned forward.

William stepped closer. "You must tell us everything."

She clasped her hands in front of her. "It was many years ago. My father said he wasn't himself while under the poison's influence. It manipulated his mind and body."

"Where did he encounter this poison?"

Leah hesitated. "The Dark Forest."

"The Dark Forest?" Elijah said with a chuckle. "That place is a myth—folklore to keep children inside the city limits."

The girl snapped her head in his direction. "It's real. I know because my father's been there. He's told me the stories and documented his experience in his journals."

"Journals?" William asked. "He made records of this poison? Do you have the journals?"

"They're at my house. I can take you to them."

Elijah nudged his horse forward. "My prince, this is surely a trap."

William glanced at him, then back at the girl.

A familiar tingling pressure formed in Theo's throat,

and before he could stop himself, he said, "We should trust her."

Leah looked past William to Theo and smiled.

"No one cares what you think, Bard," Elijah said.

William turned to Theo. "He's right. This is our only option."

Elijah sighed.

"You said your name is Leah?" Theo asked.

The girl nodded.

"Can we trust you, Leah?"

"I'm choosing to trust you," she said. "We both have something the other wants. We have no choice but to trust one another."

William glanced between Theo and Leah, then mounted his horse. "It's settled then. Take us to your home to see these journals."

Leah tossed her brown braid over her shoulder. Her green eyes flashed as she smiled and said, "Follow me."

Chapter Seven

THEO JOINED WILLIAM and his men as they followed Leah through the forest. After about fifteen minutes of navigating through dense woods, the trees thickened so much they had to stop and tie up their horses.

After leading them a few more minutes on foot, Leah stopped and said, "We're here."

Theo glanced around. "Where's your house?"

She grinned and pointed up.

"Whoa." Theo gaped at a massive tree house.

"Impressive," William said. "Your father built this?"

"With help from his wife and daughter," Leah said. She beamed proudly. "A little nicer than your cave, don't you think?" She smirked.

"We came here to see your father's journals," Conrad interjected. "Not to examine your family's craftsmanship."

"Of course." Leah unwound a rope from a nearby tree branch. It dangled before her, one end tied securely to the platform above her head, the other end dragging on the ground. "Up we go." She gripped the rope with both hands, then jumped, scaling the cord as if she'd executed the maneuver a hundred times. The sleeves of her tunic bunched around her elbows, revealing strong forearms. She reached the top and peered down at them, not even winded. "There's a ladder over there," she said, pointing to the makeshift rungs on a nearby tree trunk. "If you'd prefer." She smiled, then disappeared into the house.

"I'll go first," Conrad said. "To make sure it's safe." He scaled the ladder with little effort. William followed, then Elijah, and lastly Liam.

"Coming, Bard?" Liam asked.

Theo adjusted his lute and satchel on his shoulders, then gripped the wooden boards and hoisted himself until his boots hit the rungs. A stunning view greeted him at the top—and not just the scenery. The house was a piece of art. Woodgrain swirled on the round front door, and hollow wooden chimes dangled from a small porchlike overhang, greeting him with a melodic song. An odd arrangement of herbs hung in a bundle beside them. Theo paused to examine the leaves before entering.

William and the other rebels were already inside when Theo entered the main living space. The room was sectioned into two areas. One adorned with brightly colored pillows and a low table. The other equipped with a woodburning stove, counterspace, and jars of herbs and grains. A washbasin sat in the back corner where Leah tugged on a pulley above her head. Water released through a hollow wooden tube, filling the kettle in her other hand. She placed it on top of the stove, then retrieved mugs from a wooden shelf and began filling them with dried leaves and honey.

"Please make yourselves comfortable," she said over her shoulder.

William and his men whispered among themselves while Theo wandered the kitchen. More bundles of herbs hung from the rafters, filling the house with a fragrant aroma. Wooden shelves lined nearly every open space on the walls, stacked with rows of glass jars and clay pots.

A pounding sound drew his attention back to Leah, who was grinding additional herbs for their tea with a pestle and mortar.

His eyes drifted past her to a spiral staircase that sat in the back corner of the kitchen area opposite the wash basin.

"Tea's ready," she said, retrieving the kettle and

pouring hot water over the leaves.

William accepted a mug, but Conrad took it from him and sniffed its contents. William shot him an amused look, waiting for his second-in-command to give his approval.

Leah appeared beside Theo with a mug. "Would you like some?"

"Yes, please. Thank you." Her fingers grazed his when she handed him the mug. Warmth spread through Theo's body as he took a sip.

Leah motioned to the pillows and table in the living area. "Please have a seat," she said.

William and his men made their way over. Theo followed Leah as she joined them.

Old books sat in stacks on the floor around the perimeter of the room. Theo stared at them, his eyes scanning the titles on their weathered spines. A thought gnawed at the back of his mind. He couldn't pull his attention from them.

"You said your father brought you and your mother out here to live when you were just a child?" William said.

"Yes, when I was four."

"Why did your father flee the city?"

Leah glanced down for a moment, then joined the others on the floor. She folded her legs beneath her. "I know you described your king as a kind ruler—at least before his mind was overtaken by the poison—but King Tyrus was not so kind to my father."

Theo looked away from the books. "Why do you say that?"

"Bard, please," Elijah said. "Let the prince do the talking."

William held up a hand. "He's fine, Elijah."

Elijah set down his tea. "Are we not here to see the journals? Why are we wasting time with pleasantries?"

William shook his head. "Ignore him. Please, Leah, continue."

"Actually, this story ties into my father's journals. So your precious time shall not be wasted." She grinned at Elijah.

He softened.

"My father has always been a bit of an outsider," she began. "And as an herbalist, he traveled to many lands beyond the walls of Viren. He's as much an explorer as a healer, always in search of exotic flowers and herbs. When I was still quite young, his travels led him to the far east, across the Emerald River and into the Dark Forest, which, I assure you, is quite real."

She stood and crossed to the small kitchen to retrieve the kettle of water. When she returned, she began topping off each of their mugs.

"It was there my father encountered the poison you described. The toxin clouded his eyes and mind and filled even the air he breathed. He worried the poison would one day breach the Emerald River and reach the city of Viren." She paused as she poured the hot liquid into William's mug. She held his gaze. "It seems my father was right."

William shifted.

"I'll let you read the details in my father's journal, but suffice it to say, he made it out of the forest alive. Upon his return to the city, my father sought audience with King Tyrus to warn him of the Dark Forest and the threat it held for any who entered. The king was deeply upset and feared my father would frighten the people—and for no reason. So the king branded him a madman, knowing that no one would dare to listen to the ramblings of a madman. Shortly after that, my father brought my mother and me out here to live in the wilderness as far away from the Dark Forest as we could travel."

Theo's mind spun with the words of her story. "If what you say is true, then Marsuuv must be from the Dark Forest."

"An interesting thought, Bard," William said. "But we can't know that for sure."

Theo sipped his tea. "It makes sense, though. No

one knows where he's from."

Conrad cleared his throat. "Forgive me, but I'm with Elijah on this. I've heard stories of the Dark Forest, but I was always told they were folklore."

Leah set the kettle to the side. "Then why would it be forbidden to go there?" She waited, but no one responded. "It's not forbidden because it's fantasy." She held Conrad's stare. "It's forbidden because it's real."

Theo shifted, feeling an unsettling chill despite the hot drink.

"It's forbidden because it's forbidden," Elijah interjected. "Just as it's forbidden to enter another's kingdom or marry someone's betrothed. These are the ways of our people."

Leah shifted. "My father always said Viren's superstitions would be their doom."

"You're not superstitious?" Theo asked. "I saw the herbs at your front door: dill, lavender, oregano, and parsley—bound with a figure-eight knot and adorned with a sprig of sorrel. A bouquet said to ward off curses."

Leah stared at him a moment before answering. "My father isn't superstitious, but my mother is."

Elijah stood. "Enough of hexes and wards. Show us these journals."

"Of course," Leah said, making her way to the spiral staircase.

Theo jumped to his feet. "I'll help you."

"I'm sure the girl doesn't need help lifting a couple books, Bard." Liam chuckled.

The sound of the rebel men's laughter followed them up the stairs.

Theo watched Leah's feet ascend the steps ahead of him. She wore handmade leather shoes, similar to moccasins. They made no sound as she climbed.

"The house has three levels," she said. "The first is our kitchen and living space, as you saw." She paused on the stairs as they passed through the second level. "Here's where we sleep. And upstairs," she continued climbing, "is my father's study." She stepped into the room at the top level.

"Whoa." Theo followed her into the space, his eyes scanning countless books, stacks of papers, quills, and ink wells. The scent of dust, leather, and dried ink stirred his mind with sparks of something familiar, but he couldn't place it.

"This is where my father does his journaling." She ran her fingers over a worn wooden desk. "As a little girl, I wasn't allowed up here. He worried I would misplace something."

"It looks like everything is misplaced," Theo said.

Leah chuckled. "To you, yes, but to my father, everything is right where it should be." She crossed to a bookcase lined with leatherbound journals, pulled one down, and thumbed through its pages. "When I began my studies, I was finally allowed up here." She returned the journal to its place.

"Your studies?"

"I'm my father's apprentice," she said proudly.

"You're an herbalist too?"

"I am." She scanned the books and journals as if searching for a particular one. "Oh, here it is."

She stood on tiptoes and with great care removed one of the journals from the shelf. A bright red cord wrapped around the brown leather cover and held the pages closed. "As his apprentice, I have access to all of his books and journals except this one." She smoothed her hand over the cover. "This one details his time in the Dark Forest."

"You weren't allowed to read it?" Theo asked. "Wouldn't that make you want to read it even more?"

She glanced up at him. "Of course it did. But I wouldn't dare. I love my father and respect his wishes. He's my teacher, my mentor," she paused, "my closest friend …" Her eyes drifted back down to the journal. "I must admit it feels like betrayal to read it now." She paused and chewed her lip. "But my parents' lives depend on it."

She said nothing more as she passed Theo and

descended the stairs, clutching the journal to her chest. She walked straight over to William, who now stood in the kitchen area. She stopped before him, then hesitated, eyes staring into his.

"Remember, we agreed to trust one another," he said.

Theo noticed the way she lifted her chin ever so slightly before handing the journal to him.

"Thank you." William dipped his head, then began thumbing through the pages. Theo and the other rebels joined them in the kitchen.

"His drawings are exquisite." William turned the journal around and pointed to an ink sketch of a plant Theo had never seen. A strange looking piece of black fruit dangled from its vines. "Is this entire journal about the Dark Forest?" William asked.

Leah nodded.

"Is it his *only* journal about the Dark Forest?"

"It is."

"Hmmm …" William continued flipping through the pages.

Leah approached Theo and spoke in a low voice. "Did you like your tea?"

"It was delicious." This close, he could see the flecks of gold in her deep-green eyes.

Her full lips flickered into a smile. "It's my own recipe."

Theo held her stare for a moment longer than felt appropriate. He couldn't shake the feelings her eyes evoked. The color stirred his mind, reminding him of something familiar he couldn't put his finger on.

"Here!" The sound of William's voice interrupted the moment. He jabbed at the page with his finger, then began reading aloud.

"From the moment I entered the Dark Forest, I felt the slight shift in my awareness—a clouding of my mind and vision. The toxic effects overtook me slowly, drawing me in subtly so I didn't know I was being infected. Until I did.

"In my delirium, a strange white creature approached, telling me to eat a specific variety of white lily to clear my mind. To this day, I don't know if this creature was real or a concoction of my imagination, but nonetheless, its instructions saved my mind. However, they didn't protect my body. I overstayed my welcome and was chased from the forest by monsters darker than I care to remember. Foul-smelling batlike beasts with black wings and devilish red eyes attacked me and pierced my flesh with their sharp talons. I escaped with my mind and my life, but I was not unscathed."

William paused, then continued.

"In all my travels, I have never encountered a

toxin as venomous as Malum, nor have I ever seen its peculiar antidote—the white lilies of the Dark Forest.

"Now, I write of the events as if they were a fever dream. But I know they're real. My body bears the marks of the dark beasts to prove it. And now it feels my duty to warn the world of this very great and present danger."

William stood silent for a long moment, then closed the journal. He pressed a hand to its leather cover. "So there's an antidote." He peered up at them. "We must find it. We have to save the king."

"Yes, there's an antidote," Leah repeated, "but it only grows in the Dark Forest."

"My prince, you can't seriously be thinking about a journey to the Dark Forest," Conrad said. "It's forbidden."

Leah stepped forward, eyes on her father's journal. "Sometimes we must do what is forbidden."

Theo suspected she still felt a hint of guilt at having shared her father's journal with strangers.

"The girl is right," William said. "We're going to the Dark Forest. Bard, take Leah back to our camp. The two of you will stay with our people until my men and I return."

"That's kind of you to offer," Leah began, "but I must insist that I go with—"

Theo held up a hand to cut her off. The familiar sensation returned in his gut, pressure that forced its way upward into his throat. A tingling sensation accompanied it. Words formed on his tongue, and before he could think, he said, "We should go with you."

William stared at him, but no one spoke.

Theo continued. "Leah is an herbalist too, trained by her father. She should go with you. Her skills could be useful."

"And you?" William asked.

"Haven't I proven myself useful once before?"

The prince's expression didn't change. He finally frowned. "There's something about you, lad. Fine. Gather your things, young Herbalist. And quickly. It's three days' ride to the Dark Forest from here."

He crossed the room and exited the front door. Conrad, Elijah, and Liam followed.

When they were out of sight, Leah turned to Theo and said, "I can't believe he agreed to bring us along. That didn't take nearly as much convincing as I thought."

The tingling in Theo's throat subsided. "Yeah. I'm surprised too."

"I guess you really do have a way with words." She smirked. "I'd better pack my things. I'll join you in a moment."

Theo watched her climb the stairs. He touched his

throat. "I guess I really do," he whispered to himself as he turned to leave the tree house.

Inside a small tent, Theo quickly changed his shirt. He sniffed the dirty one, winced, then stuffed it inside his satchel. Crickets chirped outside and firelight flickered on the canvas. They'd been traveling for a day and a half, covering two days' worth of travel in record time. William had been pleased with their progress, and they were set to descend upon the Dark Forest before evening the following day.

Theo pulled a clean shirt from his satchel and paused before pulling it over his head. In the dim firelight through the tent wall, he could make out the five marks on his arm. His stomach flipped when he realized only four were as they had been. Only the outline remained of the fifth.

"They're fading," he whispered to himself. "I'm running out of time."

But even as he said the words, Theo didn't know how he knew these things.

He tugged his shirt over his head, pulling his sleeves all the way down to his wrists, then checked to ensure the bars couldn't be seen through the fabric.

If William and his men realized that Theo was cursed, they wouldn't dare bring him along—especially on their journey into the forbidden Dark Forest.

He pushed the thought from his mind, grabbed his lute, and returned to join the others around the campfire. Taking a seat across from Leah, he strummed a couple of chords. She didn't even look up, her eyes glued to the pages of her father's journal, which lay open in her lap. Her soft brown hair fell around her shoulders in thick waves left behind from her braid. He watched the firelight play across her face, then asked, "What are you reading about?"

She glanced up. "Fruit. My father's writing suggests there are many kinds in the Dark Forest. Fruit I've never seen or heard of before. It's fascinating."

Liam burst from his tent in a clean tunic and pants. "Ah yes, much better. Now I don't stink quite so bad." He stretched, then plopped down on the log beside Theo. "What do you say, Bard? Play us a tune?"

Theo glanced at Leah. "Oh I don't know—"

"Come now, Bard, your angelic voice is one of your few useful skills. And we are weary travelers."

Elijah, Conrad, and William filtered out of their tents and joined them.

Theo caught Leah staring. "I'd love to hear your angelic voice," she said in a teasing tone.

Theo had never felt embarrassed to sing before, but Leah's presence made him nervous.

Elijah interlocked his fingers behind his head and leaned back. "Yes, Bard, sing us a song or we'll be forced to declare you un-useful and will have no choice but to leave you here."

Theo forced a smile, then strummed his lute. He hummed along at first, finding the right tune as his fingers deftly picked the strings. He closed his eyes to shut out the stares of the rebel men and, more specifically, Leah. As he did, tightness formed in his stomach, then a warm pressure that pushed toward his throat. The strange tingling sensation returned, filling his lungs and propelling music from the depths of his soul.

A song of hope formed on his tongue, lyrics filled with memories from home and a promise of brighter days.

He felt tears well behind his closed eyes as his own words carried him back to his mother's arms and his father's companionship. The longing for his parents intensified. The grief for their absence pierced his heart. And once again, he felt as if he'd already lost them. He sucked in a deep breath, pushing through the lament with his song. Finally he concluded, holding the last note and strumming the final chord.

Silence lingered in the wake of his song. He opened

his eyes, glancing first at Liam. Tears glistened on his cheeks. Beside him, Elijah bit his lower lip and nodded. Conrad sat silent, eyes closed, while William stared at an open locket in his hand, which, Theo guessed, contained a picture of Princess Rosaline.

He looked at Leah last. Tears brimmed in her green eyes. She clutched her father's journal to her chest. "Beautiful," she said.

The presence of William and the other rebels faded from Theo's awareness until it felt as if only the two of them remained.

"Beautiful," Theo repeated. But unlike Leah, he wasn't speaking of the song.

She grinned, then looked away, staring into the flames.

But her smile lingered.

Chapter Eight

THEO STOOD BESIDE LEAH, staring across an old, rickety bridge. Moss covered the broken boards, reflecting the deep-green color of the narrow river that flowed beneath it. Daylight faded, streaking the sky with dusky purples and blues, deepening the greens of the forest on the opposite side of the river. The peak of a mountain ascended above the tree canopy in the distance.

Theo broke the silence. "I can see why it's called the Emerald River."

William and the other three rebels approached the waterline, staring down into the gentle flowing stream.

Beside Theo, Leah removed her father's journal from her satchel and flipped through the pages. "This is it—the Dark Forest," she said. "But it looks nothing like what my father described."

William turned from the river to face her. "What do you mean?"

She stepped toward him, showing him the open pages. "He wrote about black, leafless trees and dying vegetation. But look." She pointed to the woods on the other side of the riverbank. "This forest looks as vibrant as the one to the west of Viren."

William took the journal from Leah and skimmed a few pages. "Odd. Perhaps he was wrong about the details."

Leah snatched back the journal. "He's not one to miss details."

William made his way to the bridge. "Let's hope he's right about the antidote." He gripped the dry-rotting handrails and placed a cautious, booted foot onto the planks.

"Of course he is." Leah stuffed the journal into her satchel and pushed past Conrad to cross the bridge ahead of him and Elijah.

"After you, Bard." Liam motioned for Theo to go next.

He straightened his shoulders and stepped onto the bridge. The wooden boards groaned beneath his feet. Leaning to the right, Theo peered past Elijah and Conrad to see Leah following directly behind William. She'd pulled her hair back into another braid and wore a clean tunic and pants. Somehow, despite two and a half days of travel on horseback, she still managed to look put-together. And, Theo had noticed, she still smelled good.

"Interesting," Liam said behind him.

"What?" Theo asked, glancing over his shoulder while still minding his footing.

"Her." Liam nodded his head at Leah.

Theo felt heat rise in his cheeks. "What about her?"

Liam's eyebrows darted up. "You tell me." A grin lingered on his face.

"I don't know what you're talking about."

Liam chuckled. "Perhaps you're not so unfamiliar with the ways of love."

Theo ignored him, crossing the final few slats of the bridge onto solid ground. He froze when he took in the scenery.

Leah gasped. "Look!"

Not even twenty paces in front of them, the once vibrant-green forest now towered above them with dark and ominous trees. Black trunks soared into the dusky sky, topped with gnarled, bare branches. Beneath their feet, leaves decomposed into dark soil. The scent of mildew hung in the air.

"He was right," Leah said, her voice barely above a whisper.

Conrad drew his sword with his right hand, then reached into his pocket with his left. He pulled out a knotted cord with five stones attached—all shades of red and gold. Theo recognized the charm right away. His mother had given him one as a child. In his haste, he'd forgotten to pack it when he'd fled the city several days ago.

Conrad gripped the good-luck piece in his left hand, then stepped toward the Dark Forest. "Let's go."

William unsheathed his weapon and followed his second-in-command. "Eyes open. Stay alert."

Elijah crossed himself, placing a palm on his forehead, chest, then each shoulder. He drew an arrow from his quiver and readied his bow.

Liam's smile had faded, replaced by a look of deep concern. He motioned for Theo and Leah to go ahead of him.

Leah drew her hunting knife. "Don't you have a weapon?" she asked Theo.

He shrugged. "I guess I can use my lute if I have to. But I'd rather not."

"Keep up," Elijah called back to them. "We don't want to get separated."

The forest exhaled cold air as Theo stepped inside the tree line. A chill slithered down his spine. He placed a hand on Leah's shoulder, then stepped in front of her, feeling that he should go first.

The earth gave way silently beneath his boots,

too soft to make a sound. Black thorny vines snaked between the trees, catching on his vest and tugging at his sleeves. He tucked his arms closer to his body, not wanting to tear his shirt and reveal the dark secret that branded his skin.

Behind him, Leah sniffed. A moment later, he caught a whiff of a peculiar scent. "What's that smell?" he asked.

Leah coughed. "It smells like rotting flowers."

The scent became more pungent the deeper they ventured. About a hundred yards in, the air grew colder, but a searing heat burned across Theo's right shoulder. The black marks on his arm burned and itched with every step he took. He restrained himself from scratching, not wanting to draw attention to Marsuuv's curse.

Tightness formed in Theo's chest, but not the tingling pressure he'd grown familiar with over the past few days. Opening his mouth, he sucked in a labored breath, then coughed. Tension pounded in his head. A chill raced up his spine and spread across the back of his skull, clouding his mind with a foggy feeling. He stumbled, catching himself on the trunk of a tree. Behind him he heard Leah fall to the ground. She called his name, but it sounded muffled, drowned out by the beat of his own heart in his ears.

Ahead of him, someone vomited, but his vision was

too blurry to see who it was.

"What's happening?" Leah mumbled.

Theo turned to look at her. His vision swam; a heaviness overtook his body, dragging him to his knees. He flopped down and rolled onto his back, then saw a flash of white streak through the sky.

"A bird?" Theo mumbled.

The creature swooped low, circling Theo's body like a vulture. It was a furry bat, not a bird. The image of it stirred his mind, as if he'd seen this creature before. "Poison," he muttered, now realizing what was happening.

The giant bat landed on the ground beside him. Reaching out with a winged arm, it wrapped its fingers around his wrist and pulled. The motion felt familiar, but Theo couldn't place it. His mind swirled as he sat up with the bat's assistance.

The creature peered at him with wide green eyes, then said, "Quickly, you must come with me. To the white lilies." It tugged again, yanking Theo to stand on unsteady feet.

"You talk?" Theo managed to stammer.

"Yes, yes, yes, but first lilies. We'll talk later."

The bat pulled again.

"Wait." Theo reached behind him and grabbed Leah by the wrist, dragging her along with him as he stumbled behind the creature into a tiny circular clearing. White lilies bloomed along the perimeter, filling the air with their intoxicating scent.

"Eat," the bat commanded. "It'll clear your head."

Theo dropped to all fours and plucked the nearest flower. Without thinking, he shoved the entire bloom into his mouth and chewed. A rich, honeylike flavor covered his tongue. Within seconds, the fog in his brain subsided. After eating a second, his vision cleared. He ate a third, and the world stopped spinning. Sighing, he turned to see Leah seated on the ground beside him, slowly chewing. A moment later, William and the other rebels stumbled into the clearing and began gorging themselves on lilies.

They sat in silence for several minutes before Theo spoke. "It looks like Leah's father was right."

"Right about what?" the creature asked.

They all turned to stare at it.

"I can't believe it," Elijah said. "I thought your father was crazy. But unless my eyes still deceive me, *that* is a talking bat."

"A bat?" the creature chuckled. "No, no, no." It patted its chest with its wings. "I'm a Roush. And my name is Sebastian."

"It has a name?" Liam chuckled, then burst into hysterical laughter. He popped another lily into his mouth. "Clearly I'm still under the toxin's influence," he said with garbled words, "because I thought it just said its name was Sebastian."

The Roush shrugged. "Well, it is."

Theo watched the creature with curiosity and a strange sense of familiarity. "Thank you," he said to it, as if it were completely natural to have a conversation with a talking, mystical creature. "Thank you for leading us to the white lilies. You saved us."

"Saved you? Oh no, no, no." The Roush shook his head. "I *guided* you. That's all my programming allows me to do—advise and encourage."

Theo narrowed his eyes, confused by the Roush's words. "Well, thank you for guiding us, Sebastian. It's nice to meet you. I'm Theo."

The Roush waddled closer. "I know." It winked a green eye at him.

"You know—"

A loud groan interrupted Theo's question. William rose on wobbly legs. "Clearly we were intoxicated by the poison of this dark place."

"Malum," Sebastian said. "It's what we call the poison."

"I remember reading that in my father's journal," Leah said. "He entered the Dark Forest many years ago. Perhaps you remember him. His name is Marlowe."

"Oh yes, I remember him. My, my, my, he was in quite a state when I found him. Worse than all of you combined."

"And this is the lily you gave to him as well?" Leah asked.

"Yes. And it cleared his mind as it did yours. It's a powerful plant."

"So this is the antidote for the poison then?" William asked, plucking a flower. "A dark stranger called Marsuuv entered our city and poisoned our king. We believe he used this Malum. If we take these flowers, will they cure him?"

"Marsuuuuuv," The Roush drew out the name. "Yes, yes, yes, bad news indeed. One of the darkest creatures this forest has spawned."

"So he is from here?" Theo asked.

 Sebastian nodded.

"It must be the Malum then," William twirled the flower between his fingers. "Grab as many flowers as you can carry," he said to his men. "Quickly, we must use these to heal our king."

"Hmmm …" Sebastian mused. "The white lily is a powerful healer, but I don't know for certain that it will save your king." He tapped his chin as if thinking.

"Well?" William asked. "Will it or won't it?"

"Here, look." Leah opened the journal and showed

Sebastian her father's drawing of the plant that saved him. "Is this the same lily?"

"Oh yes, yes, yes. That's it."

"So it *is* the antidote?" Leah asked.

"For your king?" The Roush shook his head. "That I don't know."

"We don't have time for this," Elijah muttered. "Let's get the flowers and get out of here. Clearly these are the same ones the herbalist's father wrote about in his journal."

William and his men focused their attention on plucking flowers and filling their satchels. Sebastian turned to Theo and smiled. Behind the Roush, Leah wandered off into the nearby trees.

"So, a Roush?" Theo asked.

Sebastian nodded.

"What exactly is a Roush?"

"What's a Roush?" The creature chuckled. "Well, what exactly is a human?" He laughed harder, as if he'd made a joke. He composed himself, then said, "A Roush is a costume just as a human is a costume."

"I don't understand."

"Not to worry, young Theo. You will." The Roush winked again.

Theo stooped and plucked another flower and began eating it, thinking his mind was still under the effects of the Malum.

When the Roush didn't disappear, he asked, "So you're real?"

"As real as everything else."

The phrase tickled Theo's mind. "Are there more of your kind in this forest?"

"There are very few Roush here. Very, very, very few. And not the ones you've previously met on your other adventures."

"What other adventures?"

"Oh, I've said too much." Sebastian swatted his own hand. "Bad, bad, bad. I'm only here to guide you. He warned me to be careful not to say too much."

"Who warned you?"

"Never mind that. There is much more I must tell you." Sebastian stood straighter, extending to his full height of about two feet. "Now, while there aren't many Roush in the Dark Forest, there are *many* Shataiki. Many, many, many."

A shiver worked its way through Theo's shoulders, but he didn't know why. "Shataiki?" he repeated.

"Oh yes. Surely the young lady's father must have included a note about them in his writings."

A picture filled Theo's mind as he recalled the words William had read from Leah's father's journal. "Foul-smelling bats?" he asked. "Giant wings? Red eyes? Terrible talons?"

"Yes," Sebastian nodded. "Horrifying creatures, though, I'm not afraid of them."

"You're not? Why? They can't hurt us?"

"Oh, they can hurt you, but only inside the confines of this Dark Forest. They are powerless to leave, slaves to their dark lord, Teeleh. Only Marsuuv can leave the bounds of the forest."

Theo's head swam with the information. He waved William over. "William, you need to hear this." Leah and the other rebels joined.

"Tell them what you told me," Theo said to Sebastian.

"The Shataiki aren't able to leave the forest, just as Teeleh isn't able to leave."

"Shataiki?" William asked. "Teeleh?"

"I'll catch you up," Theo said. "Go on," he urged Sebastian. "What were you saying about Marsuuv?"

"Marsuuv is the only creature who can leave the Dark Forest. And he can't kill a human."

Everyone froze, eyes glued to the Roush.

"Tell me everything you know about this Marsuuv," William said.

"He is evil," Sebastian said, "but he's merely an emissary for the one who rules this place, the dark lord, Teeleh. *He* is the real threat."

Theo saw William's expression shift. "Grab more

lilies," he commanded his men, then pulled Theo aside. Over the prince's shoulder, Theo saw Leah approach Sebastian with her father's journal. The Roush spoke to her in hushed tones, pointing at words and drawings on the pages. Leah paced back and forth as she listened, rubbing her shoulder, then fidgeting with her braid.

"What else did the Roush tell you about Marsuuv?" William asked Theo.

"Only what you just heard. But we must move quickly. The beasts Leah's father described are real, and …" A loud rustling interrupted him.

Silence fell over the forest as William, Theo, Leah, and the others all stopped and listened.

Sebastian peered up into the trees. "Speak of the devils."

Three large bat-shaped images perched on a bare branch, silhouetted against the dusky-blue sky.

Theo stared at the red eyes of one glaring directly at him. It blinked, then stretched out its large, tattered wings. The one beside it screeched. More black bats began to settle on the bare branches above the first three. A dozen, at least.

Conrad lifted his sword. "I think it's time to leave," he whispered.

Elijah nocked an arrow and aimed into the branches. "I've got this."

"I wouldn't do that if I were you," Sebastian said.

"Then what would you do?" Theo asked.

The Roush turned his green gaze from the Shataiki, stared at Theo, then said, "Run."

Blood turned to ice in Theo's veins.

"Now!" the Roush urged. "Quickly! They can't harm you on the other side of the river."

"Let's go!" William shouted. He ushered Leah and Conrad ahead of him. Liam and Elijah sprinted on their heels.

"Let's go, Bard!" Elijah called over his shoulder.

But Theo stood frozen in place.

Sebastian grabbed the hem of his tunic and tugged. "You must go! Hurry, hurry, hurry! Oh, and Theo …" The Roush's small hand wrapped around his wrist. "You may have found the white lilies, but don't forget what you truly seek." He paused. "You may find it here."

The Roush shoved him in the direction of the others, then took to the sky. "Run!"

Theo caught up to the rest of his group as they burst through the tree line and onto the riverbank. He skidded to a stop behind Leah.

"What are you waiting for?" Theo demanded. "Run! Across the bridge!" He pushed past Leah to the front of the group.

A Shataiki blocked their path, wings outstretched. It

leaned forward and hissed at Theo. A sulfurous stench wafted off its matted black fur and heavy breath.

Another Shataiki landed beside it, narrowing its red eyes.

A third took up position to that one's left.

Then another.

And another.

And then a hundred as if all at once.

Chapter Nine

FIERY HEAT BURNED across Theo's right shoulder. He could feel the markings of his curse as fresh as the moment he'd been branded, as if the hex was responding to the presence of the dark beasts. Every pair of red eyes stared directly at him.

Behind him he heard William shout, "Weapons at the ready!"

Theo didn't move, wishing he had more than a lute to use for protection. He fumbled for the instrument's strap on his shoulder, dreading the idea of wielding it but knowing he had no other choice.

"Hold still, Bard!" Elijah shouted.

Theo heard a bowstring being pulled taut.

Another wave of Shataiki landed in front of him.

Then more.

The creatures blanketed the riverbank, leaving no empty space to run.

The one nearest to Theo released an ear-piercing

shriek, then stepped forward with a taloned foot. A cacklelike sound rippled through the horde of monsters. The Shataiki at the head stepped closer. The two on either side of it closed in.

Theo took a step backward, overwhelmed by the stench and the swell of terror that flowed through his veins.

The closest Shataiki beat its open wings and shrieked again, revealing drool-covered fangs.

Terrified, Theo stumbled backward, caught his heel on a stone, and fell to his seat. A scream slipped from his mouth, leaving a tingling sensation on his lips.

The three stalking Shataiki froze and stared. Their ears flattened against their heads like those of a frightened dog.

"Theo!" Leah shouted from behind him. "Get up!"

The Shataiki in the center shook its head, then lurched closer.

Pressure bubbled in Theo's gut, pressing upward. He felt as if he was about to vomit, but then the tingling sensation returned, filling his lungs, burning in his throat.

He pushed up on one elbow, seeing the Shataiki's talons mere inches from his own foot. He leaned forward, staring straight into the beast's eyes, and screamed.

Again the Shataiki's ears flattened against its head. It backed away, snarling. The monsters behind it shuffled backward.

A whistle pierced the air. Theo looked up, following the sound. Sebastian sat in the boughs of a tree, peering down at him.

"Sing, boy! Use the gift within you. Sing!"

Theo snapped his attention back to the Shataiki. They stood frozen, as if waiting for him to make his next move.

The pressure in his lungs swelled. Fire burned in his throat. Theo couldn't hold it much longer. He pushed himself up to his feet.

The entire mass of Shataiki shrieked in protest and moved closer, beating their wings like a war drum.

"Theo!"

He turned to see Leah, eyes wide, body trembling.

"Sing!" Sebastian shouted again. "Release your power!"

Turning back to the monsters, Theo sucked in a deep breath, placed the palm of one hand against his chest, and opened his mouth. A clear, crystal tone poured from his lips, resonating from the depths of his being.

The Shataiki trembled as if they were glass vessels ready to shatter.

Theo took a step forward, raising the volume of his voice, then the pitch.

The Shataiki shook their heads and grasped at their ears with spindly fingers.

"Run!" William shouted.

Leah took off first, passing Theo. He didn't dare move as William and the rebels darted around him toward the bridge. He planted his feet, holding the note as if his life depended on it.

Because it did.

Fighting against the wall of sound Theo hurled their way, the Shataiki lashed at Leah. Talons dug into William and the other rebels' flesh as they pushed through the wall of beasts.

Theo took a step forward, raising his volume once again.

Unable to withstand the power of his song, the black batlike creatures parted before him, many leaping for the skies.

He could see the bridge. His friends raced across the weathered planks, rushing to the other side.

Theo's lungs burned with the fire of his song. He couldn't hold the note much longer. Digging deep into his diaphragm, he pushed every last ounce of air through his vocal cords and sprinted toward the bridge.

Shataiki nipped at his back, grasping with taloned

feet, snapping sharpened fangs. Every inch of his skin burned, but he pushed forward.

Just before his foot hit solid ground on the other side, one of the Shataiki swooped low, slashing his right shoulder, then dragging its claws down to his forearm. The impact knocked Theo to his knees. He crawled across the final few planks of the bridge and collapsed against the soft grass. His left hand flew to his shoulder, gripping the bloody wound. When he pulled his fingers away, he saw that the Shataiki had ripped his shirt, slashing the skin directly beneath the markings on his arm.

Two and a half bars remained.

Before anyone could see, he quickly ripped the sleeve from his shirt and tied it around his wounded bicep and shoulder.

Panting, Theo rose to his feet and faced the bridge. From this side, he could no longer see the Shataiki, only green trees and lush forest. Even the Roush was gone.

He turned back around to find five pairs of eyes staring at him.

Blood trickled down William's forehead and into one of his eyebrows.

Leah clutched a gash on her left thigh.

Conrad, Liam, and Elijah appeared similarly wounded.

But everyone still stared.

William finally broke the silence.

"How'd you do that?"

Theo swallowed, the pressure now gone from his lungs and throat. He touched a bloody hand to his lips, then said, "I don't know."

Chapter Ten

THE DARKNESS OF MIDNIGHT filled the sky, broken only by faint moonbeams that sifted through thick clouds. Several hours had passed since the events at the Emerald River. Without so much as a word, William had led their group away from the water's edge back to their horses, which they'd left tied up on the other side of the river. The prince had mounted his horse in silence, eyes fixed on Theo, then led their group several miles into the deep woods before stopping to make camp. Despite the Roush's warning that the Shataiki couldn't cross to the other side of the river, William wanted to distance themselves from the Dark Forest.

Now, they lingered around a campfire, chewing jerky and tending to their injuries, but William still hadn't spoken to Theo since the riverbank.

The rebel men sat opposite Theo. Leah stood in

front of them, offering a salve she'd created for their wounds. After treating them, she made her way over to Theo and took a seat on the log beside him.

"You're hurt," she said, taking his right hand in hers. She flipped it palm up, exposing the deep, gnarled gash that wrapped from the inside of his forearm up to his shoulder where the makeshift bandage remained.

"Just a scratch," Theo said.

"It's deep. You should let me treat you." She placed her pestle and mortar on the log beside them. A green goo glistened inside the bowl.

"It's okay." He pulled his hand away. "I already wrapped the worst part."

Leah ignored him and reached for his hand again. Before he could protest, she rubbed the salve into the exposed wound.

A warm tingling sensation spread over his skin beneath the balm, followed by a gentle force, as if someone were placing pressure on the gash. The pain dissipated.

"Wow, this feels incredible. Is this one of your father's recipes?"

"Herbalist," Liam said, interrupting their conversation.

"She has a name," Conrad chided.

Liam shrugged. "What's in this salve? It's as if my

wounds are healing before my eyes."

Leah wiped her hands on her pants, leaving green smears. "Oh, nothing special. Just something I whipped up."

"Your own recipe?" Theo asked.

But before she could answer, Conrad spoke up. "And you, Bard. I still don't understand how you used your voice like that. What are you, some kind of magician?"

William shifted beside Conrad, fixing his eyes on Theo. "Why didn't you tell us you have this kind of power?" the prince asked. "What else are you keeping from us?"

Theo averted his eyes and stared into the flames. His mind drifted to the fading marks on his arm.

"Come now, don't be bashful, Bard," Liam teased. "We knew you had the voice of an angel, but we didn't know you had a vox to slay devils."

"Vox?" Theo asked.

Elijah rolled his eyes. "It means 'voice' in the old language. You youths really know nothing of our traditions."

Liam extended his arms in front of him, taking stock of his salve-covered injuries. "Now that we know of the bard's gift, he and his vox should lead us into the city to destroy Marsuuv and liberate the king."

Theo shifted. "Oh, I don't think that's a good idea."

Liam slapped his hands on his thighs. "And why not?"

Theo fumbled. "I mean, this is all new to me. I don't know if it will work on Marsuuv—or if I can even do it again." When he glanced up from the flames, William was staring, his face unreadable.

"Of course you can. Let's practice," Liam said through a mouthful of jerky. He jumped to his feet and brushed his hands on his pants. "Use your vox to make me dance."

Elijah smirked.

"Liam, please," Conrad protested. "Leave the boy alone."

"No, no, I'd like to see this." Elijah leaned back. "Go on, Bard. Use your vox to make Liam dance."

"I don't know—"

"Oh, come now, this will be fun. Let's see just how powerful you are." Liam positioned himself several feet from the fire.

Theo shook his head, then took a deep breath. He waited for the pressure to form in his belly and throat. But nothing happened. So instead, he opened his mouth anyway and let out a note. It came out slightly off key.

Elijah chuckled, but Liam stood still, eyes closed,

hands at his sides as if he were a puppet preparing to be animated.

Theo cleared his throat and tried again. He held the note for only a couple of seconds before clamping his lips shut. "This is stupid. I'm not doing this anymore."

Liam burst into laughter.

William shook his head. "Sit down and leave the bard alone. He did just save our lives, after all."

Liam's grin faded. He returned to his seat. "Forgive me, Bard. I was merely trying to have a little fun after escaping certain death."

"Yes, well, you should be thanking him, not asking for his forgiveness," William said. "His gifting may not work on fools like you, but it was most certainly our salvation today with those beasts." The prince paused and held Theo's stare. "And who knows what else he's capable of. You were right, Bard, you've proven yourself to be quite useful to the rebel forces."

Theo nodded absently.

"Thank you," Liam said in a serious tone.

"Yes, thank you, Bard," Conrad said, dipping his head.

Elijah stood and rounded the fire to stand before Theo. He extended a hand to him. Theo hesitated, then reached out to clasp Elijah's forearm as he'd seen William do with his men.

"Thank you," Elijah said. "You saved our lives. For that, we owe you our own." He returned to his seat. "So thanks to the bard and the herbalist, we now have the antidote for King Tyrus. Now what do we do?"

"The only thing we can do," William said. "We sneak into the city and administer the antidote."

"And how do you suggest we do that?" Conrad asked. "There's a bounty on your head—ours too."

"I know of a farmer who lives on the outskirts of the kingdom," Liam said. "We could borrow a cart and enter the city under the guise of making a delivery. I'm confident he'd help us."

"That'll never work," Elijah said. "We're members of the King's Guard. And he's Sir William Atwood. They'll recognize us immediately."

"*Former* King's Guard," Conrad corrected. "But you're right. We will certainly be recognized."

Leah straightened beside Theo. "I can help."

The rebel men turned their attention to her.

She stood. The waves of her unbraided hair flowed softly around her shoulders, but her posture was firm. "No one in the entire city will recognize me. I haven't been there since I was four years old."

William leaned forward, resting his forearms on top of his knees. "Go on."

"I'll drive the cart," she said. "You and your men can hide in the back."

William's eyes drifted to the fire. His face remained still, but Theo knew his mind was not.

"It's too dangerous," he finally said. "You're just a girl—" William caught himself. "You're quite a capable young lady, but I can't in good conscience put you at that kind of risk."

Leah folded her arms over her chest. "You have to."

William flashed a smile, but his tone was firm. "I'm the future prince of Viren. I don't have to do anything."

Leah tilted her head. "You do if you want the antidote to work."

William's forehead creased. "And why do you say that?"

"Because I spoke to the Roush and pressed him for details about the lily."

Theo recalled seeing her speak to the creature alone.

"Sebastian told you he didn't know if the flowers would work without being preserved," Leah continued. "So he gave me a recipe for a tea using the lilies and a few other ingredients that will help them retain their power. It's our best shot for administering the antidote successfully."

William straightened. "And let me guess: you won't share this recipe with us?"

Theo saw the corners of Leah's lips flicker upward. "I'll make the recipe if you take me with you."

William sighed. "It'll be dangerous."

"I know."

The prince nodded. "It's settled then. You'll drive the cart."

"And the bard comes too," Leah quickly added.

William waved her words away. "His parents were recently taken captive. You may not be recognized, but he will."

"I'll wear a disguise," Theo offered. "She's right. I should go too. Besides, wouldn't it look more suspicious to see a young woman driving a cart into the city on her own?"

Leah shot him a look.

Theo held up his hands in defense. "*I know* you're not just a girl, but the guards at the gate don't."

Her face softened. "Good point."

"I'm also familiar with the city," Theo added. "She'll need help navigating."

"Another good point," Leah said, facing William.

"And then there's my vox," Theo added. "I can be useful."

William flashed a stern look. "You wouldn't be trying to use your voice on me now, would you, Bard?"

"No, I …"

William cracked a smile, then sighed. "It seems both youths will be joining us."

"Lovely," Elijah said, the sarcasm evident in his voice.

"Actually, Elijah, one of us should ride back to camp

and inform the others of our plan. Besides, I find it unlikely that four full-grown men will fit into the back of a farmer's cart."

"Say no more," Elijah said. "I'll leave for the caves at first light."

"Thank you." William bit into a piece of jerky. "Now, Herbalist, did the Roush share other important information that you've been keeping to yourself?" He raised his eyebrows. "We're in this together now. It's best to not keep secrets."

Leah lifted her chin, then took a seat. "As a matter of fact, he did." She crossed her legs.

"Well then, out with it," Conrad urged.

Leah removed her father's journal from her pocket. She flipped to the back. "There were a few empty pages, so I made a note of it here."

"Did you also write down the recipe for the antidote?" Liam asked.

Leah covered the pages with her arms.

"Relax, Herbalist," William said. "You're going with us."

She paused, then uncovered the pages and read. "Sebastian said, 'Malum is a powerful toxin but not nearly as powerful as the poison that flows in a human's veins.'"

"What does that mean?" Theo asked, glancing over her shoulder.

"Human blood is poison to Shataiki. When our blood mixes with theirs, it's deadly to them."

Theo leaned back.

"Well that would have been nice to know a few hours ago," Conrad said. "Why didn't you tell us?"

Leah slammed the journal closed. "First, I wasn't exactly thinking clearly while being threatened by hundreds of giant rabid bats. Second, what would you have liked me to do? Slice open my palm, dip arrows in my blood, and shoot them?"

Liam shrugged. "Not a bad idea. We should return to the Dark Forest and eliminate the threat."

"There are far too many," William said. "We leave for Viren at first light. Our mission is to save the king. We'll not waste time with flying rodents."

"But—"

"That is the plan," William said, cutting off Liam before he could protest again. "Now, let's enjoy our meal, and perhaps later the bard can play us a song."

"Not much of a meal," Liam said, biting into a piece of jerky.

The rebels lowered their voices as they chatted amongst themselves.

Leah shifted beside Theo and returned her father's journal to her pocket.

"Is there really an antidote recipe?" he asked.

She faced him on the log. "Yes."

He nodded. "It was smart to keep it to yourself."

She flashed him an infectious smile. "I thought so too."

Theo held her gaze until he felt uncomfortable. He looked away.

"How's your arm?"

Theo had forgotten about it. He glanced down. "Whoa." He turned his wrist until the firelight illuminated the now barely visible wound. The skin had closed, leaving behind a thin pink line. "It's healed." He lifted his gaze to meet Leah's. She stared at his arm, wide-eyed.

"How'd you know to make this salve? It's a miracle balm."

Leah shook her head. Under her breath she uttered, "I—I don't know. It just came to me." Her green eyes pierced his. "How'd you know to sing like that back at the river?"

Theo pressed his lips together and swallowed. "I don't know. It just came to me."

Leah nodded.

"Hey, can I get a little more of that salve? I want to change the bandage on my shoulder."

"Of course," she said. "Need help?"

"No, thanks. I've got it."

Theo scooped some of the green paste into his palm, then made his way to his tent. Once inside, he removed his shirt and untied the strip of fabric from his shoulder. The gouge beneath the black bars pulsed, the skin red and inflamed. He rubbed the balm into the wound, feeling an immediate tingle of relief. The strange pressure sensation came next, reminding Theo of the feeling in his throat and lungs as he sang at the riverbank.

He stared at the black bars, noting that two were empty, and the third was only a quarter of the way full.

"I'm running out of time," he whispered to himself. He furrowed his brow, "And becoming more powerful."

He traced a finger over the black outlines of the two empty bars.

"Marsuuv," he said, his voice low. "A man of shadows. A man from the Dark Forest." He paused, remembering something the Roush had said. "And perhaps not a man at all."

Theo smoothed the salve into his skin, watching the wound draw together, closing before his eyes. He considered Leah's words when he'd asked her how she'd known to make it.

I don't know. It just came to me.

Just as the song had come to him.

His mind lingered over the thought for a moment, then pushed it away. He changed his shirt, grabbed his lute, and returned to join the others around the fire.

Chapter Eleven

THEO PULLED HIS CLOAK TIGHTER around his shoulders and adjusted the hood on his head, drawing it closer to his face. The towering walls of Viren loomed in the distance. Leah shifted on the seat beside him in the cart, her knuckles white as she gripped the horses' reins. They hadn't heard a single sound from William, Conrad, or Liam who hid beneath the false bottom in the back with stacks of hay bales above them.

"So that's Viren," Leah said, breaking the silence.

"No," Theo said, his voice low. "That isn't Viren. That's Marsuuv's domain."

Leah shot him a sideways glance, then turned back to the dusty road. She shivered and slid closer to him.

At his mention of Marsuuv, the burning on his shoulder felt hotter and he was reminded once again that he was running low on time. They had to get in and out of the city so he could find a Waystation, or the curse would kill him when the bars on his arm ran out of life.

"Can you pick up the pace?" he asked Leah.

She hesitated. "What? You're eager to throw yourself into the jaws of the lion?"

"No, but the sooner we get in, the sooner we get out."

She nodded. "Yeah." And she urged the horses to keep a steady pace.

A few minutes later, they neared the main city gate. Theo straightened his shoulders and adjusted his cloak once more, feeling a chill run through his body. The soaring walls of the city appeared taller than he remembered, their previously majestic stone façade now cold and threatening. Even the once vibrant vines that snaked across the city walls looked dull and lifeless.

Two men stepped out from a small guard shack near the main entrance and crossed to the center of the road. The gate remained sealed behind them. One of the guards held up a hand, commanding them to halt.

Leah pulled the horse to a stop. She glanced around nervously, wiping her palms against the skirt of the plain cotton dress she wore. She'd complained about it at first but gave in when William insisted it's what a farmer's daughter would wear. Theo had almost told her how nice she looked in the dress, then thought better of it when he saw her tugging at the long billowy sleeves in frustration.

The midday sun beat down on them as they waited for the guards to approach. A bead of sweat ran down Theo's back beneath the cloak. He swallowed against the dryness in his throat, noticing the familiar green and gold uniforms of the King's Guard as they made their way to the front of the cart.

Leah's leg pressed against Theo's. He could feel her tremble.

"State your name and business," the guard demanded.

Leah cleared her throat, but when she spoke her voice sounded strong and confident. "Good afternoon. My name is Leah. I have a delivery for the royal stables."

The other guard walked around to the back of the cart to inspect their cargo. The guard questioning them asked, "And which farm are you from?"

"Arthur Wesley's. I'm his daughter."

The guard's eyes scrutinized her face. "Why would he send his daughter to make his delivery?"

Leah lifted her chin, meeting the guard's intense stare. "We had a cow go into labor this morning."

"And your father has no sons to do his work for him?"

Theo kept his face fixed straight ahead, but from the corner of his eye, he saw the muscles in Leah's jaw clench. "My brother was recently injured in a plowing accident." She forced out a fake smile. "But my father respects his duties to the king and wouldn't dare delay his delivery. So he sent me."

A loud thump sounded in the back of the cart. The second guard had climbed inside to conduct a more thorough search. Theo held his breath.

"And who is this?" the guard asked, gesturing to Theo.

"Our stable boy," Leah quickly answered. "You'll have to forgive his silence. He's deaf and mute, but he's quite capable of helping me unload the hay. After all," she chuckled in a fake tone, "I'm just a girl."

"Of course," the guard said. He stepped toward the back of the cart, drew his sword, and stabbed a bale with his blade. Theo and Leah exchanged glances. "Well?" he asked his comrade.

"Looks clean to me." The inspector jumped down from the cart.

The first guard returned and handed Leah a piece of parchment. Theo noticed King Tyrus's seal at the top.

"If anyone questions you, just show them this document so they'll know you've already been cleared for entrance."

"Why, thank you," Leah said in an artificially sweet tone.

The gates swung open. Leah snapped the reins and

navigated past the guards. Once through the main entrance, she exhaled loudly.

"That was so nerve-wracking."

"You did great," Theo said. "You know, for a girl." He grinned.

Leah punched him in the arm. "I can't believe I had to degrade myself like that." She made a gagging sound. "My father would be horrified."

Theo shifted to a more serious tone. "No, he'd be proud of you."

Leah softened. "Thank you."

The sound of horses hooves against cobblestone accompanied them down the main city road. Recognizable storefronts greeted Theo, all featuring green stained-glass windows. But their vacant doorways were not so familiar. The normally bustling streets of Viren sat quiet and empty. A rancid stench greeted them when they passed one of Theo's favorite produce vendors. Rotting fruit lined the stands of Mr. Dietrich's storefront. A sign hung on the emerald-green window saying Closed Until Further Notice.

Farther down the road, a couple of women huddled together, cloaks drawn tight over their heads. Upon hearing the approach of Leah and Theo's cart, they scattered, disappearing into darkened vine-covered alleys.

"What happened here?" Leah asked. Her shoulder pressed into his.

"Marsuuv happened," Theo said, his eyes glued to the gothic tower that rose from the skyline in front of them. He pointed. "That's the university." He paused. "Where my father taught."

Leah placed a hand on his leg. "I'm so sorry about your parents."

Theo slid his hood back so he could see her more clearly. "I'm sorry about yours too."

Leah returned her gaze to the road. "Which way to the stables?"

"Just follow this street past the university."

The royal residence became visible as they rounded the school.

"There." Theo pointed.

"There?" Leah's eyes widened. "It's a castle."

"What did you expect?"

Leah shook her head. "I don't know, but I miss the forest."

Theo's eyes scanned the five green glass spires that rose from the palace compound like sharpened swords. He swallowed. "Right now, so do I."

Leah navigated the cart down one of the palace's service roads.

"There," Theo said, pointing to lush green fields dotted with tiny red flowers. A pristine white building sat in the center, glowing in the afternoon sun. Horses grazed nearby, lazily swatting flies with their tails. And a boy about their age emerged from the main stable building, carrying a sack of feed over his shoulder. He watched Theo and Leah approach, then pointed to a smaller outbuilding, indicating where they should make their delivery.

Leah snapped the reins, urging the horses forward. She pulled to a stop outside the small stone building. A moment later, the boy arrived.

"Documentation?" he said, while slumping the bag of feed onto the ground.

Leah flashed him the paper.

The boy nodded, then gestured to the stacks of hay in the back of the cart. "Unload it here. Do you need a hand?"

Leah pointed to Theo. "I have all the help I need."

"Good." The boy hoisted the bag of feed and continued on his way.

Theo slid down from the front seat of the cart and stepped into the outbuilding. Cool air greeted him inside the stone shed along with the scent of hay. Bales lined the perimeter of the building, stacked several feet over his head.

Theo returned to Leah. "There's no one inside. Back the cart up to the doorway, and we'll start unloading."

He tossed his cloak to the side and made quick work

The Boy and His Song

of unloading their cargo. Leah joined him, complaining under her breath about the impracticality of dresses and how men had surely designed them to make women's lives miserable.

Theo smiled, grateful for a distraction from the fact they'd illegally entered the city and were about to break into the palace.

Finally they'd cleared the floor of the cart. Theo scanned their surroundings before removing the boards of the false bottom.

Liam gasped as he sat up. "Finally, fresh air."

Conrad groaned as he climbed out.

William exited last, looking as regal as ever. "Good work, you two."

"Now what?" Leah asked, picking hay from her braid.

William peered around the cart at the wide-open fields. He glanced at the sun high in the sky. "When we were King's Guard, the staff tended the horses in the morning and at night. Let's hope that's still the case." He pointed to the large white building. "There's a drain at the back of the stable. From there, we can access the main palace." He scanned the field one more time. "On my word, we run for it. Ready?"

Theo wanted to say no, but then he saw Leah beside him, gripping the hem of her dress in her hands, prepared to sprint.

"Now!" William said, taking off across the field toward the stables.

Conrad and Liam followed closely behind their leader. Theo sprinted behind Leah, feeling both impressed and intimidated by her speed. The horses barely glanced at them as they passed.

Behind the stables, the ground sloped away from the building toward a large metal drain cover.

William and Conrad gripped the grate and lifted.

"Oh my—" Leah covered her mouth with her hand. Her eyes watered. "You can't be serious. It smells awful."

Liam lowered himself inside first. "I thought you weren't too girly to get dirty." He released the ledge and dropped down into the darkness with a splash.

Leah fought back a gag, then pushed past the other rebels. "Dirty, I don't mind," she said while climbing into the drain. "But smelly?" She shook her head. "I still have my dignity. You boys could all take note of that." She held her breath, winked at Theo, then dropped into the drain.

"After you, Bard," William said.

Theo splashed into the drain, followed by William and Conrad. He pulled the collar of his shirt over his nose to try to block the overpowering scent of manure.

"Just hold your breath," William said. "We'll be past it shortly."

Liam and Conrad pulled the grate closed behind

them while William took the lead, guiding the group down a dark, damp tunnel. After about a quarter of a mile, they stopped.

"Conrad, Liam, help me with this." William pointed to a large, rusted circular grate on the right side of the tunnel.

"What's that?" Theo asked.

Conrad drew his sword and smashed a bolt with the hilt. "An access point to the old sewer system." He grunted. "It hasn't been used in years."

The metal groaned with a loud echo as the rebel men pulled the grate from the opening, then set it to the side. William hoisted himself into the five-foot opening first, crouching low. "Let's go."

A deeper darkness greeted them inside the tunnel.

"Stay close," William said. "It'll be dark, but it's a straight shot. Just keep moving forward."

A thump echoed through the passage.

"Ow!" Liam groaned.

"Quiet," Conrad said.

Theo stepped forward, following the sound of splashing feet in front of him. Within several yards, the scent of manure faded, replaced by an overpowering odor of mildew and rust.

They traveled in silence for what felt like twenty minutes before William's voice called back to them. "We're here."

"How can you tell?" Theo asked. But when he stepped forward, he saw the dim light seeping into the tunnel from above, illuminating the rusty curved walls.

"The palace dungeons should be right above us."

Theo shifted, thinking of his parents. "How do you know the dungeon won't be filled with Dark Riders?"

"We don't," William said. Torchlight from above flickered over his chiseled facial features. Theo could read the intensity in the prince's eyes—an intensity that would face any danger to free his beloved Rosaline— the same passion that had propelled Theo's every move since the moment his parents were taken captive.

"When we were King's Guard," Liam explained, "prison duty was usually a quiet station. Then again, we didn't have many prisoners."

Theo swallowed.

"Will we see them?" Leah asked. "My parents?"

"No," William said. "This drain leads to the prison but not the cell block."

"*Can* we see them?" Leah clarified. "Can I check to see if they're even here?"

William didn't answer, already sliding the drain cover aside. He hoisted himself out, followed by Conrad and Liam, who helped to lift Leah and Theo into the torchlit stone tunnel.

"Stay here," William commanded, pointing to Theo

and Leah. He and the other two rebels crept silently down the tunnel, then followed the passage to the right.

Sounds of a scuffle reached them. Leah jumped, grabbing hold of Theo's arm. She quickly released him. "C'mon," she said, jogging down the tunnel.

They rounded the corner to find William, Conrad, and Liam crouched over an unconscious and bound Dark Rider. William pulled a set of keys from the guard's belt, then nodded to a barred metal door to the left. "That's how we get into the palace." He pointed to a wooden door on the opposite side of the tunnel. "That leads to the cell block." He stood and unlocked the wooden door. "You two have two minutes." He swung the door open.

"Thank you!" Leah rushed past him.

Theo hesitated, then followed.

Barred cells lined both sides of the hallway, cramped with citizens of Viren. Theo's throat constricted as he entered. Pressure formed behind his eyes. At the end of the hallway, Leah sobbed, clinging to the bars of one of the cells. A woman and man reached through from the other side, also crying.

"Thank Elyon you're here," her father said while cupping Leah's face.

The phrase caught Theo off guard. "Elyon?" he whispered.

"Theo!"

His father's voice. Theo spun toward it.

Halfway down the hall, his father and mother peered around the other prisoners, stretching their hands toward him.

Theo ran to them. Tears streaked his cheeks. But he froze at their gaunt appearance when he neared them. Breath caught in his throat.

"Mom?" His voice cracked. "Dad?"

"My boy," his mom said.

"Hey bud." His dad smiled.

Grief stabbed Theo's chest. His eyes searched the faces of his parents. "It's you," he breathed. "It's really you." The familiarity of their faces awakened the anguish in him. He blinked. "You're here. You're real. You're ..." His voice quivered. "You're alive." He rushed to the bars, reaching his fingers through to touch them. "I thought I'd lost you forever. It felt like—it felt like you'd died."

"Oh, Theo." His mom held him through the bars. The sound of her voice saying his name struck him as if he was hearing it for the first time. He pulled away, wiping his cheek with his sleeve. He met his father's stare, somehow feeling the sorrow even deeper.

"I'll get you out of here. I promise."

"William!" Leah's voice interrupted.

Theo looked to the left, seeing William enter the cell block through the wooden door. "Time's up. We need to move," he said.

"Give me the keys!" Leah demanded. "Give me the keys so I can let them out! All of them. They can escape through the sewers!"

William stepped toward her, clenching the keys in his hand. "Not now."

Intensity burned on Leah's face. "Yes. *Now!* Give me the keys!"

"Then what?" William asked. "There are at least a hundred prisoners here. We can't sneak a hundred people out of the city in the middle of the day. If we let them out now, we're ensuring their deaths. We must first save the king." He fixed her with his stare. "And I need you for that. You have the antidote."

Tears poured down Leah's cheeks. "The king has already ensured their deaths—a week from today. Their sentence has been set." Her lips trembled. "All of them. They're going to kill *all* of them."

Theo turned to his parents. "Is this true?"

His father nodded.

"But not now," his mother said, hope brimming in her eyes. "You're here to save us."

"If we save the king, we save them all," William said. "We *will* come back for them. I promise."

Leah bit her lip, but a sob still escaped. She ran back to her parents, clinging to them through the bars, whispering words through her tears.

"Say your good-byes," William said to Theo. "For now. You will see them again. Of that, I am certain."

Theo clung to his parents' hands. Their touch awakened memories in his mind, some familiar, and others he didn't recognize, as if they were dreams of his parents in another life.

"Let's go." William tugged on his arm.

"Mom. Dad. I—"

"I know," his mother said. "We love you too."

William pulled Theo down the hall, but Theo watched them over his shoulder, feeling with every step that he was losing them forever.

A new pain stabbed his chest. The pain of having lost, then found, then lost again.

He pushed the thought from his mind, clinging to the belief that, somehow, a greater hope remained—the hope of being united with them once again.

Chapter Twelve

WILLIAM CLOSED THE DOOR to the cell block. Leah pressed her hands against the wood, tears still streaking her cheeks.

Theo placed a hand on her shoulder.

A loud smack drew his attention back to the rebels. Theo watched as William slapped the prison guard across the face a second time. The guard mumbled and moved. Conrad pulled him into a seated position and leaned him against the stone wall.

"Where's the king?" William demanded. "And tell me what you know of Rosaline? Where is she?"

The guard screamed. "Intruders!"

William clamped a hand over his mouth.

Conrad drew his sword, then placed the tip against the guard's neck.

"Let's try this again," William said. "Where is the king?" He slowly removed his hand from the guard's mouth.

"William," the guard said, his voice low and threatening. "There's a reward promised to the man who delivers your head to the king. A very large one." His eyes darted to the other two rebels. He tried to smile. "Conrad and Liam, it's been a while, my friends. Your heads may be handsome, but they aren't worth as much as the prince's pretty face."

Conrad pressed the sword harder against the guard's neck, drawing a thin line of blood.

William held up a hand.

Conrad huffed and removed the sword but kept it aimed.

"I'll ask you one more time," William said. "If you don't provide an answer, I'll have no choice but to search the entire palace myself—and leave Conrad here with you. Alone. Surely you know his reputation?"

The guard's eyes darted from one rebel to the next.

"Where is the king?" William asked, enunciating each word.

The man's jaw muscles clenched. He leaned his head back against the stone wall, staring straight ahead with a look of defiance.

"Kill him," Leah said, her voice quaking with emotion. "Kill him!"

Theo grabbed her arm and pulled her back.

"Look what he's done to our parents!" she cried.

"Get her under control!" Conrad demanded.

Theo pulled her away from the interrogation.

When she spun on him, the look in her eyes unsettled every nerve in his body, awakening a fire in Theo's veins. It spread toward his gut, then erupted upward. Before he could stop himself, Theo spun, crouched before the guard, grabbed him by the collar of his uniform, and in a low voice said, "You're going to tell me everything you know about the king." Theo's throat tingled. "Where is he?"

The guard's eyes widened. His jaw fell slack. "In his study," he said.

Conrad straightened, sheathing his sword.

"That's where he spends most of his time now," the guard explained. "The king only comes out when he's ready to retire to his private chambers. But even that's hearsay. No one has seen him in the last week."

"And where's the princess?" Theo asked, feeling his lungs burn.

"I don't know. No one has seen her since Marsuuv arrived. Most of the King's Guard believe she's no longer in the city."

"What do you mean she's not in the city?" William demanded.

The guard's gaze drifted to the prince. He spat to the side, then clamped his lips shut.

"What do you mean she's not in the city?" Theo repeated in a voice barely above a whisper. He could feel William's eyes on him but refused to meet his stare. Instead, he focused on the electrifying energy that pulsed in his gut, up his throat, and onto his lips.

"It's rumored she's with Marsuuv's dark lord," the guard said. "But I—"

William shoved Theo aside, grabbed the guard by the shoulders, and yanked him to his feet. "Tell me how to get to her! Where is the dark lord keeping her?"

Conrad placed a hand on William's shoulder. "We don't have time for this now. We must get to the king."

William's face twitched, but he didn't release the guard.

"If we save the king, we can save Rosaline."

"We need to move now while the coast is still clear," Liam added.

William dropped the bound guard. The man slumped to the ground, groaning.

Conrad used the hilt of his sword to knock him out. "He won't be going anywhere." He sheathed his weapon and shrugged. "And now he can't scream."

William's lips pulled into a tight line. He produced the key ring once again, this time reaching through the barred metal door to the left to unlock it. "Bring our friend," William said, holding the door open for Liam and Conrad to pass through, carrying the guard. "Bard, Herbalist, let's go."

Leah turned for one last look at the wooden door that led to the cell block.

"We'll be back for them. You have my word."

Leah looked at William, then to Theo. "We're running out of time," she said.

"C'mon." Theo grabbed her by the arm and pulled her through the door.

William fixed his cool eyes on Theo as he passed. "Your vox was quite useful. Again."

Theo dipped his head. "It was my honor."

"Stay close, Bard," William said, pulling the door closed. "Who knows what else your vox may be able to do."

On the other side of the barred door, Conrad and Liam shoved the unconscious guard into a closet. Torchlight flickered in the small hallway, illuminating a stone stairway to the left.

William waited for his men to secure the guard, then said, "Fortunately this palace has many hidden passages—the kind only a princess and her betrothed would know about. Follow me."

After several minutes of leading them through the winding hidden corridors of Viren's palace, William finally stopped to shift a large wooden structure at the end of one of the halls. Firelight crept in from the other side. The prince slipped through first, then motioned for the others to follow through the doorway, which Theo discovered was disguised as a bookcase on the other side. They stepped into the dimly lit study.

Shelves lined every wall, covered with countless books. The scent of aged paper stirred Theo's mind. He hesitated beside the fake bookcase, his fingers grazing the spines of the ancient manuscripts. A layer of dust lingered on his fingertips.

Light pierced his eyes as William drew back one of the window shades. Theo blinked and turned to see a cloud of dust settle to the floor.

"I've never seen his study in such a state," William said, gazing around the room.

"It smells like death," Liam said.

As he said it, a stale, sour smell reached Theo's nostrils, and the sound of a raspy, strained breath filled the room.

They all turned toward the source.

In the darkest corner of the room sat a wooden rocking chair, and on it, the crumpled form of an old man, facing the corner.

"My lord," William said, rushing to him. He spun the chair around.

Leah followed, removing a white lily from her satchel.

King Tyrus's greasy white hair lay plastered against his scalp. His matching beard was long and unkempt. A black blindfold covered his eyes. His chin slumped against his chest.

"My lord?" William said.

The king didn't speak, but his chest rose and fell with another labored breath.

"My lord, it's me, William—Rosaline's betrothed."

Theo followed Conrad and Liam as they joined William.

"My lord? King Tyrus?" William removed the blindfold from the king's face.

Leah gasped and backed into Theo, blocking his view.

He grabbed her shoulders to steady her. "What's wrong?"

Her voice trembled. "His eyes."

Theo stepped around her.

King Tyrus's head remained slumped. Saliva glistened on his lips, while his solid black eyes stared straight ahead at nothing.

Chapter Thirteen

THEO COULDN'T LOOK AWAY from the king's dark, hollow stare. An inky blackness filled his eyes, the whites completely blotted out by the effects of the Malum. William knelt before him, shaking his shoulders, but Tyrus gave no indication that he knew the prince was there.

"Quickly, Herbalist," William said, interrupting Theo's thoughts. "The antidote!"

Leah tugged on Theo's sleeve. "Help me."

He followed her across the study to the fireplace.

"Give me your flask," Leah demanded. She found an iron kettle and stirred up the embers in the hearth.

He handed her the full canteen, watching as she poured the water into the kettle, then placed the pot directly on top of the coals. Pushing past him, she emptied the contents of her satchel onto a nearby desk, placed two of the large flower blooms into the bowl of her pestle and mortar, and began grinding.

"Hand me that little pouch, will you?" She nodded her head at a tiny leather drawstring bag the size of a coin purse. "Pour the contents in here as I grind."

Theo followed her instructions.

"Great, now find me a cup."

Theo crossed the room, seeing a tea set on a side table near the door. A thin layer of dust coated the china. A book lay open beside the tiny cup. Theo brushed his fingers over its cover.

"Hurry!" Leah called.

Theo returned with the cup.

"Grab the kettle." She pounded the flowers and herbs a few more times, then scraped the fine powder into the teacup. "Great, now pour the water."

A fragrant steam rose from the cup as the hot liquid mingled with the ingredients of the antidote.

"Are you almost finished?" William asked.

"Ready," Leah said, carefully carrying the steaming cup to the king. She handed it to William. "It's hot but not too hot."

Conrad and Liam pulled the king upright in his chair while William forced the warm liquid past the king's lips. He coughed but swallowed.

"All of it," Leah said. "He needs to drink all of it."

"I'm working on it," William said, trying to ensure

the liquid ended up in the king's mouth and not on his chin. Finally, he poured the last few drops into his mouth.

King Tyrus's throat bobbed as he swallowed.

"Now what?" William asked.

"We wait," Leah said. "If this works, it won't take long."

"*If* it works?" Liam asked.

"Like the Roush said, there's no guarantee it will cure him."

King Tyrus coughed violently, jerking in his chair. "H-hello?" his voice rasped.

William knelt in front of him. "My king, can you hear me?"

The blackness dissipated from the king's eyes like fog rolling off a river.

"William? Is that you, my son?"

William's face split with a smile. "My lord, you can see me?"

"Of course I can see you." The king touched William's face with a tentative hand. "Though I feel as if I'm waking from a dream. What happened?"

William stood, pulling the king to his feet. "A terrible tragedy has befallen your kingdom, my lord."

The king glanced around the room, his now clear eyes landing on Theo and Leah. "Tell me everything."

Minutes after William finished explaining to King Tyrus that Marsuuv had poisoned him and kidnapped his daughter, they were following Viren's ruler through the giant wooden doors of the throne room.

"Marsuuv!" King Tyrus shouted, his now strong voice echoing off the marble floors. "Show yourself!"

Silence responded, punctuated only by the sound of their footsteps as they descended the aisle toward the throne.

"Where is everyone?" Conrad asked.

"Something doesn't feel right," Liam said. "Are there no guards at this station?"

"Guards!" the king called.

Dim light filtered in through the green stained-glass windows that lined both sides of the throne room, filling the chamber with a murky, haunting glow. Dusk descended upon the Kingdom of Viren.

"Hurry," William said to his men. "Let's search the antechamber."

The three rebels turned and marched back down the aisle.

King Tyrus lingered in the center, staring straight ahead at the throne.

An altarlike setting lay nestled in the front right

corner of the throne room, complete with flickering candles and burning incense. A large book sat open on the center of the ornate table. Theo crossed the room, feeling drawn to it. He stopped when he reached it, grazing the pages with his fingertips. Words written in the old language of Viren filled the book. Theo couldn't read them, yet still they spoke to him.

"A book," he whispered, then shook his head. "What is it about books?"

"Theo!" Leah appeared at his side, gripping his arm. "Where are the guards? We need to get out of here!" Panic flickered on her face.

"What do you mean? Everything's fine. William will find the guards and—"

"No!" Her fingers dug into his bicep. "You don't understand. I can't be here anymore!" Her eyes drifted over his shoulder. "I'm running out of time …" Her words faded. "What's the king doing?" She pointed.

Theo turned. Not fifteen feet from them, the king stepped onto the dais, approaching the throne. A perfectly round piece of black fruit sat on the emerald-green cushion.

"Theo …" Leah said. "What is that?"

King Tyrus picked up the fruit and sniffed its skin. Turning to face the aisle of the chamber, he brought it to his lips.

Theo's mind whirled. He rushed toward the throne. "King Tyrus! Stop!"

Before he could reach him, the king sank his teeth into the fruit's soft flesh. Black juice dribbled down his chin and into his ragged beard.

Theo halted, watching as a dazed expression washed over the king. Blackness filled the man's eyes. The fruit slipped from his fingertips and splattered against the marble, filling the room with a sickeningly sweet smell.

A sigh escaped King Tyrus's lips as he slumped into the seat of his throne wearing a satisfied expression, arms draped over the sides of the chair.

"William!" Theo shouted, his feet frozen in place. "William! Get in here!"

Seconds later, the pounding of booted feet sounded behind them. Theo and Leah spun to see William and his men frozen just inside the throne room doors. They descended the aisle slowly, eyes fixed on the king.

"My lord?" William said. Confusion etched his face.

Conrad placed a hand on his leader's shoulder. "William, we need to go."

William pointed. "His eyes … The antidote worked, but …"

Conrad gripped the prince's shoulder. "Clearly Marsuuv's power over the king is greater than we imagined."

"I have a terrible feeling about this," Liam said. "It feels like a trap."

"No," William breathed. "We have to do something. Herbalist! Give him more tea!"

"It won't work," Theo said, remembering the look on King Tyrus's face as he stared at the strange black fruit. "The King's under a spell, influenced by Marsuuv's dark power. All the white lilies in the world can't save him now."

Liam blocked William before he could rush down the aisle. "The bard's right. It's too late for the king now. We need to go."

William stepped back from Liam, glancing over his shoulder at the king, who stared at him with solid black eyes, a subtle grin lingering on his juice-covered lips.

"Bard! Herbalist! Let's go!" Conrad shouted down the aisle as he turned to run out. Liam grabbed William and pulled him toward the door.

"C'mon!" Theo said to Leah as he rushed to follow them.

In the halls of the palace, Theo could see the rebel men twenty yards ahead, rounding a corner.

"Keep up, Bard!" Liam called back. "To the dungeon—out the same way we came in!"

Theo's lungs pulled at the air. He pumped his arms, sprinting to catch up to William and the others.

"We can't lose sight of them!" Leah said, pulling ahead of him as she rounded the corner. "We'll never find our way out!"

A long hallway stretched before them, vaulted ceilings above, white marble below. Every footstep echoed as they ran. A row of arched windows sped past them on the left, the intricate details of their green stained-glass designs a blur.

Leah pulled even farther ahead of Theo. He'd never seen anyone run so fast, never seen anyone look so panicked.

A sharp pain stabbed Theo under his ribs. "Ah!" He stumbled, then regained his footing.

Leah didn't stop.

He pushed himself to catch up.

The rebel men sprinted, now not more than fifteen yards ahead of them.

"Down here!" William shouted and pointed to a wide descending staircase to the right. He and his men slowed to make the sharp turn.

A flash of black dropped from the ceiling directly in front of Leah.

She screamed, backing away from the cloaked man who now stood in the hallway, separating them from the others. She turned and ran to Theo's side.

Theo's eyes flickered to the ceiling, but he didn't

have time to figure out where the pale man had come from. The stranger approached. The hem of his black cloak swished around his ankles. A hood partially hid his face, but Theo didn't need to see the man's features to know who he was.

"Marsuuv," Theo whispered. Fire seared his right shoulder. The black markings of his curse burned in the presence of their master.

"Bard!" William shouted.

Theo saw the prince over the dark stranger's shoulder, but Marsuuv didn't even turn to look at him. William's expression suggested he wondered the same thing as Theo: Why would Marsuuv be more interested in him than William?

Leah clutched Theo's arm. "We need to get out of here!"

William started to run in their direction.

"No!" Theo shouted, holding up a hand. "Get out of here!"

Marsuuv smiled at Theo, revealing a row of perfect white teeth.

Conrad grabbed William by the shoulder.

William shoved him away. "We can't leave them here!"

A bubbling pressure welled inside Theo and surged up his throat. "Go!"

William froze, staring at him and Leah, then turned and followed Conrad and Liam down the staircase toward their freedom.

Theo shifted his attention to Marsuuv, who'd stopped a few feet in front of them.

Leah held him back. "Theo …" Her voice quivered. "The stairs are right there. I need to get out of here."

Marsuuv's eyes flickered to Leah, then to Theo, daring them to run.

Leah slowly released Theo's arm. Silence filled the hallway. Even the sound of her rapid breath ceased.

"I know who you are," Marsuuv said. His icy voice made no echo. He shifted slightly. Light from one of the arched windows to the left caught his sharp facial features, highlighting unnaturally high cheekbones and a thin, hooked nose.

"I know who you are too," Theo said, feeling the tingling pressure propel his words.

"Do you now?" Marsuuv's thin lips twitched. "Then you must also know you are powerless against me." He took a step toward them.

Theo sidestepped in front of Leah. "I know you can't kill any human. You're bound by the laws of the Dark Forest."

"And that makes you feel safe?" Marsuuv let out a chilling chuckle. "There are fates far worse than death and many who will do my biding if I so choose."

Leah gasped behind Theo. At the same time, a fiery pain cut into his right shoulder.

"You'll never find that which you seek," Marsuuv whispered.

The words struck Theo. His thoughts whirled. An image of a book flashed in his mind.

The tingle in his gut intensified, and an electrifying energy prickled at the back of his throat. A tune filled his mind, one he'd never heard before.

"Theo … I—" Panic filled Leah's voice. She stumbled behind him, catching herself on his shoulder.

Marsuuv took another step toward them.

Theo backed up, pushing Leah with him. He began to hum.

Marsuuv flinched.

Images of what had happened to the Shataiki at the riverbank came flooding back. Feeling the same swell in his body, Theo stepped toward Marsuuv. He parted his lips, allowing one single note to slip out.

Marsuuv took a step back.

Theo held the note and raised his voice, seeing the memory of the trembling Shataiki in his mind.

Marsuuv moved backward again, even though Theo made no advance. Hatred dripped from the man's face, as if the mere darkness of his presence could threaten Theo's song.

But when the tingling swell in his body poured out

of him like liquid fire, Theo knew Marsuuv couldn't come against him.

He took a step forward, raising his voice in volume and pitch.

Marsuuv winced in pain, then shook his head. He reached a thin hand to his temple.

Clenching his fists, Theo pressed them against his diaphragm, pushing out every last ounce of air he had in his lungs.

"Theo!" Leah shouted. "Look!"

Marsuuv's black booted feet lifted from the ground. First an inch, then several. The man's face contorted in pain. Black veins bulged on his forehead.

New strength filled Theo's lungs. Dropping his fists to his sides, he released the inferno of energy from his body.

Marsuuv rose a foot off the ground, then two.

The entire hallway seemed to tremble with the resonance of Theo's song. He closed his eyes and directed all of his focus on the energy vibrating against his vocal cords. A scream welled up inside him. Theo felt powerless to hold it in.

So he didn't.

Opening his eyes, he released a sound that encompassed all the emotion he'd experienced over the past week: the grief of losing his parents, the fear for their safety, the joy of reuniting with them, and the torture of having to leave them behind. He released pain on Leah's behalf, for William and Rosaline, for the king, and all Viren.

Marsuuv's body trembled, suspended in the air.

Grasping the searing shoulder of his right arm, Theo released a deeper pain into his scream, one he didn't fully understand but couldn't shake—the pain of a life he'd lived but couldn't remember. The pain of knowing who he was and having forgotten.

Theo screamed until his voice cracked.

Green glass shattered in all the windows, spraying the hallway like confetti.

Marsuuv flew backward, thrust by an unseen force. His body sailed back thirty feet and slammed into the wall at the end of the corridor, then dropped to the ground and slumped, motionless.

Theo took a hesitant step toward him. Glass crunched beneath his feet.

"Let's go!" Leah raced past Theo to the stairs.

The panic in her voice shook him from his trance.

Torchlight flickered in the darkened stairwell as he followed her.

"There!" Leah pointed. "That's the gate that leads to the dungeon. The drain's on the other side!"

Theo fixed his eyes on the barred door, squinting

to see if William had left it unlocked.

"Go!" he shouted to her.

Leah flung open the metal door. Theo darted through behind her and slammed it closed, then reached through the bars and smashed the lock into place.

Before he could yank his hand back, a force crashed into the bars, knocking him to the ground.

Theo peered up at Marsuuv, who stared at him from the other side of the door.

The man's pale fingers caressed the lock, then slowly wrapped around the bars.

"H-how'd h-he—" Leah stuttered. "No human moves that fast."

Theo didn't answer, eyes locked on the face of evil, knowing this wouldn't be the last time he saw it.

"I've got to get out of here!" Leah said, then took off down the tunnel.

Theo held Marsuuv's stare for one final second, then followed Leah down the floor drain.

Chapter Fourteen

THEO EMERGED from the sewer drain behind Leah, wet up to his ankles and nearly empty of strength. The markings on his arm under his shirt burned hot—reminding him that he was running low on life bars. He spun to take in their surroundings, seeing the walls of the city a quarter mile behind them and the forest directly ahead. Dusk lingered in the sky. He barely had time to wonder how Leah had managed to find the escape route.

He glanced down at the discreet metal drain. No one would have ever noticed it out here on the outskirts of the city. And as far as he could tell, the grate couldn't have been opened from the outside. Theo glanced up, seeing Leah sprint toward the tree line. He followed.

"We need to get to the white pine!" Theo called after her while trying to keep up. "William said to meet there if we get separated."

Leah didn't respond or stop.

Theo entered the forest a few feet behind her.

"Leah!" he called to her in a hushed voice. "Wait up!"

She paused for a second and turned to stare at him, her deep-green eyes wide, face pale. The look of horror on her face terrified him.

"Leah—"

Before he could get the sentence out, she turned and darted in the opposite direction of the white pine.

"Wrong way!" he said, trying to keep his voice low.

But she didn't stop.

He ran after her through the thick trees, struggling to keep up as she leapt over fallen logs and branches, as if she knew exactly where she was headed … Just as she seemed to know how to find their way through the city's sewer tunnels. But after several yards she stumbled, gripping the shoulder of her right arm. She didn't even look in Theo's direction when he called her name, just continued, sprinting erratically.

Fading daylight filtered through the trees. Theo pushed up the sleeve of his shirt and cast a quick glance at his markings.

He had one bar left.

Pushing his sleeve back into place, he chased Leah.

"Leah, stop!" Panic welled in him. Something was wrong. "Leah!"

She stumbled again, and this time, Theo closed the gap. He reached for her arm, but she pushed him away, staggering forward. She tripped and grabbed onto a tree for balance.

"Leah," Theo panted.

When she turned to face him, tears streamed down her cheeks.

"What's going on? Are you hurt?"

She opened her mouth to speak, swayed, then collapsed.

Theo caught her just before she hit the ground. He cradled her warm body in his arms.

"Leah!"

He pushed the hair from her face. Her eyes stared straight ahead, unblinking, then rolled back.

"Leah!" He shook her, but her body hung limp in his arms. "No, no, no, no. Please. Please don't go." Theo knelt and laid her on the ground, feeling first for a pulse. It took him a couple seconds to find the faint throb on her neck.

"Leah." He patted her cheeks. "Leah!" He shook her shoulders, then sat back on his heels. "What do I do? What do I do?"

He leaned forward, placing his cheek in front of her lips. A soft, warm breath exhaled.

"Okay, you're breathing." He did a quick scan of her

body with his eyes. No visible blood marked her dress. "She has to be hurt," he mumbled to himself.

Theo took her head in his hands and carefully searched for signs of trauma.

Nothing.

Chewing his lip, he stared at her unconscious form and replayed the events leading up to that moment.

An unsettling thought occurred to him.

He hesitated, his fingers lingering on the cuff of her right sleeve. Slowly he pushed the billowy fabric up to her elbow, then farther. A hint of a black line peeked out from underneath the fabric.

Blood drained from Theo's face. A lightheaded feeling washed over him.

He pushed her sleeve up farther, revealing a black rectangular outline.

"Oh no …"

He pushed her sleeve up all the way.

Five empty black bars lined her upper arm.

Theo's mind whirled. She was like him!

Scooping Leah up into his arms, he stood. "I need to get to a Waystation."

Theo sprinted through the forest. Leah's unconscious

body bounced in his arms, making the trek awkward and slower than he'd hoped. His feet led the way without conscious direction from his mind. Somehow he knew exactly where to go, as if the location of the Waystation had been programmed into his body the moment Marsuuv's curse had marked his skin.

So was she also cursed by Marsuuv? But how, if she'd never been to the city until today?

Either way, he knew he was nearly out of time. He didn't dare stop to look at his final dwindling Life Bar. Instead, he pushed his body harder, forcing his feet to move faster. He'd be of no use to Leah if he collapsed too. And he had no idea when that moment would occur. Or how much time he had left before Leah …

The thought of losing her was too much. He pushed it from his mind and focused his attention straight ahead. He had to keep moving.

A faint glare caught his eyes through the trees. Theo's heart fluttered. He adjusted Leah in his arms and picked up the pace. Moments later, a white structure with a copper dome appeared in a clearing. Moonlight illuminated it with a soft glow. Theo's feet slowed as he approached.

Black vines grew along the perimeter of the building and snaked up the columns that lined the exterior. His boots sank into the plush carpet of moss that surrounded the Waystation as he carried Leah toward the structure. Theo stumbled when he reached it, arms and legs burning, but he gripped her body tighter and leaned against the outer wall. A giant set of doors appeared and swung open.

Inside, he dropped to his knees, allowing Leah's body to roll from his arms and slump to the floor. Panting, he stood and stepped into the darkness. The door closed behind him.

Lights flickered and slowly came to life, accompanied by a soft mechanical hum. A strange sense of déjà vu washed over Theo. Familiarity prickled at the back of his mind. Images flashed through his brain, but none of them made sense.

And then his memory hit him like a wave.

Theo gasped and clutched his temples, doubling over as images of Florida and his grandmother came rushing back. He squeezed his eyes closed as the grief of his father's death hit him afresh. Finally, an image of Talya filled his mind along with the memory of everything the old man had said to him inside the first Waystation.

Theo opened his eyes, allowing them to adjust to the blinding white lights of the futuristic building.

"I'm in a game," he whispered.

Glancing down at his body, he noticed that he once

again wore a black T-shirt, jeans, and his signature Converse sneakers. He pushed up the sleeve of his right arm. The Life Bars were gone, even their empty outlines. He touched a cautious finger to his skin.

"Theo?"

Leah's voice.

He'd nearly forgotten about her.

"Is that you?"

He turned to respond, but the person he saw was not Leah.

A girl about his age sat on the floor, wearing skinny jeans and a sage-green tank top. Her long blonde hair hung around her shoulders in gentle waves. She stared at him with deep-green eyes the same color as Leah's. They'd been familiar then, and now he knew why.

"Annelee?"

The girl nodded, then smiled.

They were both playing the game.

To be continued in the next book
of the Dream Traveler's Game:

BOOK SIX
THE WARRIOR AND THE ARCHER

MORE ADVENTURES AWAIT

Discover the entire
Dekker young reader universe.